# Minimalist Living Philosophy In The Modern Era

xiaobu

Published by NAFISA ANJUM TASNIM, 2024.

MINIMALIST LIVING PHILOSOPHY IN THE MODERN ERA

**First edition. September 16, 2024.**



ISBN: 979-8227265845

Written by xiaobu.

# Also by xiaobu

Fate Cruel's Joke
Beneath the Billionaire's Veil
My Billionaire Boyfriend
My Ex-Husband Came Back
Shadows of Fate
Unveiling Fortunes
Entwined by Destiny
Whispers of the Third Gender
Flower Theme cake
Minimalist Living Philosophy In The Modern Era
Stay With Me

# Minimalist Living Philosophy in the Modern Era

By Xiaobu

# Chapter 1: The Weight of Possessions

Emily sat on her bed, her eyes drifting around the room, taking in the chaotic scene. Her once neatly organized apartment now resembled a battlefield, strewn with clothes, shoes, books, and countless other items that had somehow accumulated over the years. The closet doors were flung wide open, their contents spilling onto the floor in a colorful mess. Drawers had been yanked open, revealing piles of unfolded clothing and tangled accessories.

She sighed heavily, the noise almost lost amid the rustling of fabric as she shifted her weight. The feeling of being overwhelmed had been creeping up on her for weeks, but today it seemed to crash over her like a wave. Emily had always prided herself on being organized and in control, but lately, it felt like her possessions were taking control of her.

"Where did all this stuff come from?" she muttered to herself, lifting a bright pink blouse she hadn't worn in years and tossing it onto the growing pile at her feet.

Emily had always been a collector of things. Books, clothes, shoes, knick-knacks—she loved it all. Every item in her apartment seemed to tell a story, a testament to her life, her travels, her tastes. But now, as she looked around, it all felt like a suffocating weight. Her home, meant to be a sanctuary, had become a prison of her own making.

She picked up a pair of jeans, turning them over in her hands. They were a size too small—an aspirational purchase she'd made after a particularly intense week at the gym, back when she was determined to lose those last five pounds. She had never worn them. They still had

# Minimalist Living Philosophy in the Modern Era

the tags on. She tossed them aside, feeling a familiar pang of guilt and self-recrimination.

"I'll never wear these," she thought bitterly. "Why did I even buy them?"

The realization that she had been using material things to fill an emotional void hit her hard. She had always been chasing after the next thing, believing that a new dress or the latest gadget would somehow make her feel complete. But now, surrounded by the detritus of her consumerist habits, she saw that it had done just the opposite. It had cluttered her life, her space, and her mind.

She needed a change. She needed to breathe again.

Emily reached for her laptop, her fingers hesitating over the keys for a moment before typing into the search bar: "How to declutter your life." She hit enter, and a barrage of articles and blog posts filled the screen. She clicked on one at random, a piece titled "The Minimalist Revolution: Living with Less to Gain More."

The article was written by a woman named Sarah, who described her own journey from a life of excess to one of simplicity. She wrote about the freedom she had found in letting go of her possessions, the joy of living intentionally, and the peace that came from focusing on what truly mattered. Emily felt a spark of intrigue, a glimmer of hope that maybe, just maybe, there was another way to live.

She spent the next few hours engrossed in the blog, captivated by stories of people who had transformed their lives through minimalism. They spoke of the liberation that came from decluttering their homes, the clarity they found by focusing on what truly mattered, and the contentment they felt by living simply. They all echoed the same sentiment: less is more.

For the first time in a long time, Emily felt a sense of possibility. She didn't have to be weighed down by her possessions or consumed by the pursuit of more. There was a different path, a way to live with purpose and intention.

But could she do it? Could she let go of the things that had defined her for so long?

Her eyes fell on a pair of designer heels she had bought on a whim. They were beautiful, a deep red with a sleek, slender heel. But she had never worn them. They were too high, too impractical. She had bought them because they were on sale, because she had convinced herself that she needed them, that they would make her feel more confident, more desirable.

But they hadn't. They had just taken up space in her closet, a constant reminder of her impulsive, thoughtless spending.

She picked them up, turning them over in her hands. The leather was still smooth and unblemished, the soles untouched. She felt a pang of regret, not for buying them, but for what they represented: a desperate, futile attempt to find happiness in material things.

With a deep breath, she placed the heels in a donation box. It was just a small step, but it felt like a giant leap toward freedom.

For the next few hours, Emily continued to sort through her belongings, carefully considering each item before deciding whether to keep it or let it go. She found herself hesitating over certain things—an old sweater her grandmother had knitted for her, a book she had bought but never read, a necklace her ex-boyfriend had given her. Each item held memories, emotions, a piece of her past.

But as she held them in her hands, she realized that they were just that: the past. They didn't define her, didn't hold any real power over her. She could let them go and still be herself.

She set the sweater aside, deciding to keep it for now, but placed the book and necklace in the donation box. With each item she let go, she felt a little lighter, a little freer.

By the time she was done, the box was overflowing, and her apartment looked a lot less cluttered. There was still a long way to go, but she felt a sense of accomplishment, a feeling that she was finally taking control of her life.

She sat down on the floor, surrounded by the few items she had chosen to keep, and took a deep breath. For the first time in a long time, she felt at peace.

As the sun set, casting a warm glow over her decluttered apartment, Emily made a decision. She would embrace the minimalist philosophy and start her journey toward a simpler, more meaningful life. She would learn to let go of the things that didn't serve her, to focus on what truly mattered, and to live with intention.

It wouldn't be easy. There would be challenges, setbacks, and moments of doubt. But she was ready. She was ready to live more with less.

The next morning, Emily woke up feeling surprisingly refreshed. Her bedroom, now free of the clutter that had once filled it, seemed brighter, more spacious. She stretched her arms above her head, feeling a sense of lightness that she hadn't felt in years.

She got out of bed and made her way to the kitchen, brewing herself a cup of coffee. As she sipped the hot liquid, she glanced around the room, taking in the changes she had made. The countertops, once crowded with appliances and utensils, were now clear, save for a few essentials. The cabinets, which had been bursting with mismatched dishes and unused gadgets, were now organized and streamlined.

It wasn't perfect—there was still more to be done—but it was a start.

After finishing her coffee, Emily decided to tackle her wardrobe. The thought of going through her clothes was daunting, but she knew it was a necessary step in her minimalist journey. She pulled out a large suitcase from under her bed and began to sort through her clothes, separating them into piles: keep, donate, and toss.

As she worked, she found herself thinking about the concept of value. She had always believed that the more she owned, the more valuable she was. Her possessions were a reflection of her success, her taste, her identity. But now, as she looked at the piles of clothes before her, she realized that value wasn't about quantity. It was about quality, about meaning, about purpose.

She picked up a simple black dress she had bought years ago. It was one of her favorites—timeless, elegant, versatile. She had worn it to countless events, and it never failed to make her feel confident and beautiful. It was a piece that truly added value to her life.

She placed it in the keep pile, smiling to herself. This was what minimalism was about—keeping the things that truly mattered, that brought joy and served a purpose, and letting go of the rest.

The process was slow, and at times, emotional. She found herself holding onto certain items, torn between the memories they held and the realization that they no longer served her. A faded concert T-shirt from her college days, a dress she had worn on her first date with her ex-boyfriend, a pair of shoes she had bought for a job interview.

Each item had a story, a piece of her past. But as she stood there, surrounded by the remnants of her old life, she realized that holding onto these things wasn't making her happy. It was just weighing her down, keeping her stuck in a place she no longer wanted to be.

With a deep breath, she placed the T-shirt and dress in the donation pile, deciding to keep the shoes for now. She wasn't ready to let go of everything, but that was okay. Minimalism wasn't about perfection; it was about progress, about making intentional choices, about living with purpose.

As she continued to sort through her clothes, she found herself thinking about the idea of enough. She had always been driven by the desire for more—more clothes, more shoes, more possessions. But now, she realized that more wasn't the answer. More was just a distraction, a way to avoid facing the deeper issues in her life.

Enough was what she was striving for—having enough clothes to wear, enough possessions to meet her needs, and enough space to breathe and think and live. Enough was about finding balance, about being content with what she had, about focusing on what truly mattered.

By the time she was done, her wardrobe was significantly smaller, but it felt more meaningful, more intentional. Each item she had chosen to keep had a purpose, a place in her life. She felt a sense of satisfaction, knowing that she was creating a space that truly reflected who she was and what she valued.

She placed the donation pile into the suitcase and zipped it up, planning to drop it off at the local charity shop later that day. As she did, she felt a sense of relief, a weight lifting off her shoulders. She was letting go of the past, making room for the future.

After a quick shower, Emily got dressed and made her way to the living room. She sat down at her desk, opened her laptop, and pulled up the minimalist blog she had discovered the night before. She spent the next hour reading through more articles, absorbing the wisdom and insights of those who had walked the path before her.

She read about the benefits of decluttering, not just in terms of physical space, but also mental and emotional space. She learned about the importance of intentional living, and of making choices that aligned with her values and goals. She discovered the joy of simplicity, of finding beauty and fulfillment in the little things.

As she read, she felt a sense of excitement building within her. She was on the brink of something new, something transformative. She was ready to embrace minimalism, to live with less and gain more.

But she knew it wouldn't be easy. There would be challenges, moments of doubt, and times when she would be tempted to revert to her old ways. She would have to confront the fears and insecurities that had driven her to accumulate so much in the first place. She would have to learn to be comfortable with less, to find contentment in simplicity.

But she was ready for the challenge. She was ready to redefine her life, to let go of the things that didn't serve her, to focus on what truly mattered.

She closed her laptop, feeling a sense of determination and resolve. This was the beginning of a new chapter, a journey toward a simpler, more meaningful life. She didn't know what the future held, but she was ready to find out.

Emily stood up, taking one last look around her apartment. It was still a work in progress, but it was hers—a reflection of who she was and who she wanted to be. She smiled, feeling a sense of pride and accomplishment.

She was ready to embrace the minimalist revolution, to live more with less.

# Chapter 2: The First Step

Emily woke up the next morning with a sense of resolve she hadn't felt in years. The weight of her possessions still lingered around her, but the decision she made the night before had sparked a small fire of determination in her heart. She glanced at the box sitting by her closet — the single pair of designer heels she had decided to donate. It wasn't much, but it was a start.

As she brewed her morning coffee, Emily's mind raced with thoughts of what to tackle next. She recalled the stories she had read on the minimalist blog about people purging their entire homes in a single weekend. The idea sounded exhilarating but also terrifying. She wasn't sure if she could handle such a drastic change all at once. Besides, she still wasn't entirely convinced she could live with less.

She decided to start with her wardrobe. It was the most logical choice, given that she had already begun sorting through her clothes. Her closet was overflowing with garments she had long forgotten about, many still bearing price tags. She couldn't even remember the last time she had worn some of them. It was as if her closet was a black hole that swallowed everything she owned, leaving her feeling lost and overwhelmed every morning.

Taking a deep breath, Emily opened her closet doors wide and surveyed the mess. She decided to use a strategy she had read about — pulling everything out and sorting it into piles. She grabbed handfuls of hangers and began laying everything on her bed, one item at a time. Within minutes, her small bedroom was covered in a sea of clothes.

Once her closet was empty, she sat down in the middle of the pile and began sorting. She made three piles: keep, donate, and undecided. At first, it was easy. She quickly tossed aside items that were obviously worn out or didn't fit anymore. But as she moved through her collection, she found herself hesitating. A sleek black dress caught her eye — she had bought it for a party last year but hadn't worn it since. She held it up, admiring the way it shimmered in the light.

"Maybe I'll need this for another event," she thought, almost placing it back in the keep pile. But then she stopped herself. She couldn't even remember the last time she had been to a party. With a sigh, she placed the dress in the donate pile.

As the hours passed, Emily continued to sift through her clothes, each item presenting a new challenge. She came across a cozy sweater that her grandmother had given her for Christmas two years ago. It was a size too small, but she had kept it out of guilt. Her grandmother had passed away shortly after, and Emily felt like letting go of the sweater would be like letting go of her memory.

Tears welled up in her eyes as she held the sweater to her chest, memories flooding back. She missed her grandmother terribly, but she knew that holding onto a sweater she'd never wear wasn't going to bring her back. With a deep breath, she gently folded the sweater and placed it in the donate pile.

By the time she finished sorting, the sun had dipped below the horizon, casting long shadows across her room. She was exhausted, both physically and emotionally. Her keep pile was significantly smaller than she expected, but the donate pile was much larger than she could have imagined.

Emily stood up and stretched, feeling a strange mix of relief and anxiety. Part of her was proud of what she had accomplished. She had taken a huge step towards decluttering her life. But another part of her felt a deep sense of loss. These clothes had been a part of her for so long, representing different phases of her life. Letting them go felt like letting go of pieces of herself.

She decided to take a break and headed to the kitchen to make herself a cup of tea. As the water boiled, she picked up her phone and scrolled through her contacts. She remembered reading that having a support system was important when starting a minimalist journey. She needed someone to talk to, someone who understood what she was going through.

Her thumb hovered over the contact for Aaron, the seasoned minimalist she had met at the meet-up the week before. They had only spoken briefly, but she had felt an instant connection with him. He had shared his own story of transformation, explaining how minimalism had changed his life for the better. Maybe he could offer her some guidance.

With a deep breath, Emily tapped on Aaron's name and sent him a text.

"Hey Aaron, it's Emily from the meet-up last week. I'm starting my minimalist journey and could really use some advice. Would you be open to chatting sometime?"

She hit send and waited, sipping her tea nervously. A few minutes later, her phone buzzed with a reply.

"Hi Emily! I'm glad to hear you're starting your journey. I'd be happy to help. How about a coffee tomorrow afternoon?"

A smile spread across Emily's face as she quickly typed back a response. They agreed to meet at a local café the next day. With a renewed sense of purpose, Emily finished her tea and went back to her room. She grabbed some trash bags and began carefully placing the clothes from her donate pile into them. It felt good to see the pile shrink, knowing that these items would soon find new homes.

As she tied up the last bag, Emily glanced around her room. It still looked cluttered, but she could already feel a difference. There was more space to breathe, more room to think. She knew she had a long way to go, but she was proud of herself for taking the first step.

The next afternoon, Emily arrived at the café a little early. She found a quiet corner table and ordered a black coffee, deciding to skip the usual sugary latte. As she waited for Aaron, she looked around at the other patrons. Many of them were engrossed in their phones or laptops, surrounded by their belongings. She wondered how many of them felt the same sense of overwhelm that she had been feeling.

Aaron arrived a few minutes later, flashing her a warm smile as he approached the table. He was tall and lean, dressed in a simple white t-shirt and jeans. Emily noticed that he wasn't carrying anything besides his keys and phone.

"Hey, Emily! It's great to see you again," Aaron said, sitting down across from her.

"You too, Aaron. Thanks for meeting me on such short notice," Emily replied, taking a sip of her coffee.

"Of course. I'm always happy to talk about minimalism," Aaron said, grinning. "So, how's it going? What made you decide to start this journey?"

Emily took a deep breath, trying to organize her thoughts. "I guess I just got tired of feeling overwhelmed all the time. My apartment is filled with stuff I don't need, and it's been driving me crazy. I stumbled across a blog about minimalism and something just clicked. I realized I don't have to live like this anymore."

Aaron nodded, listening intently. "That's a great realization to have. A lot of people never get to that point. They just keep accumulating more and more, thinking it will make them happy, but it usually just adds to the stress."

"Exactly," Emily said, nodding. "I spent all day yesterday sorting through my clothes. I ended up getting rid of a lot, but it was harder than I thought it would be. I didn't expect to feel so emotional about it."

Aaron smiled sympathetically. "That's totally normal. We form attachments to our things, especially when they're tied to memories or emotions. It can be tough to let go, but it's important to remember that the memories aren't in the objects themselves. They're in you."

Emily nodded, letting his words sink in. "That makes sense. I guess I just need to keep reminding myself of that."

"Exactly," Aaron said. "Minimalism is as much about changing your mindset as it is about getting rid of stuff. It's about learning to live with intention and focus on what truly matters to you."

Emily leaned forward, eager to learn more. "How did you get started with minimalism? What made you decide to change your lifestyle?"

Aaron paused for a moment, reflecting. "For me, it was a combination of things. I used to be a pretty materialistic person. I thought having more stuff would make me happy, but it just made me feel empty. I was always chasing after the next big purchase, but the thrill never lasted. Then, a few years ago, I went through a really tough breakup. It forced me to reevaluate my life and what was truly important to me."

He took a sip of his coffee before continuing. "I realized that I had been using material possessions as a way to fill a void, but it wasn't working. I started reading about minimalism and decided to give it a try. I began decluttering my apartment, getting rid of things that didn't serve a purpose or bring me joy. It was a slow process, but with each item I let go of, I felt a little lighter, a little freer."

Emily listened intently, captivated by Aaron's story. "That's really inspiring. I hope I can get to that point too."

"You will," Aaron said, smiling. "Just take it one step at a time. It's not about getting rid of everything overnight. It's about finding what works for you and making changes that align with your values."

Emily nodded, feeling more confident about her decision. "That makes sense. I think my biggest challenge is going to be letting go of the fear that I'll need something later on."

"That's a common fear," Aaron said. "But in my experience, most of the things we think we might need later, we never actually do. And if you do end up needing something, you can usually find another way to get it. It's about trusting that you have enough and that you are enough without all the extra stuff."

Emily smiled, feeling a sense of relief wash over her. "Thank you, Aaron. This has been really helpful. I feel a lot better about what I'm doing now."

"I'm glad to hear that," Aaron said. "Remember, minimalism is a journey, not a destination. There will be ups and downs, but the important thing is to keep moving forward."

They spent the next hour talking about different aspects of minimalism, from digital decluttering to simplifying their diets. Aaron shared some practical tips and tricks he had learned along the way, and Emily soaked up every word. By the time they finished their coffees, Emily felt more motivated than ever to continue her minimalist journey.

As they stood up to leave, Aaron handed Emily a small notebook. "Here, take this. It's a journal I used when I first started my journey. I found that writing down my thoughts and progress helped me stay focused and reflect on what was important."

Emily accepted the notebook with a smile. "Thank you, Aaron. I really appreciate it."

"Anytime," Aaron said. "And feel free to reach out if you ever need more advice or just want to chat. We're all in this together."

Emily nodded, feeling a newfound sense of community. She realized that minimalism wasn't just about decluttering her physical space — it was about finding a deeper connection with herself and others.

As she walked home, Emily felt lighter than she had in years. She couldn't wait to continue her journey, to discover what life could be like with less. She knew it wouldn't be easy, but for the first time, she felt ready to face the challenge.

When she got home, Emily immediately set to work. She grabbed a pen and opened the notebook Aaron had given her. On the first page, she wrote:

"Day 1: The First Step"

She then began to write about her experience decluttering her wardrobe, how it felt to let go of her possessions, and the emotions that surfaced along the way. She wrote about her conversation with Aaron and the insights he had shared. As she wrote, she felt a sense of clarity and purpose. This was her journey, and she was ready to embrace it fully.

After journaling for a while, Emily decided to tackle another area of her apartment — her bathroom. She opened the cabinets and drawers, revealing a hodgepodge of half-used products, expired medications, and forgotten toiletries. She couldn't believe how much unnecessary stuff she had accumulated over the years.

Taking a deep breath, she began sorting through everything, discarding what was expired or no longer needed. She realized that she had been holding onto things out of habit, not necessity. By the time she finished, her bathroom was clean and organized, with only the essentials neatly arranged.

Emily stood back and admired her work, feeling a sense of accomplishment. She knew she still had a long way to go, but each small step was bringing her closer to the life she wanted. A life of simplicity, clarity, and freedom.

As she prepared for bed that night, Emily felt a calmness she hadn't felt in a long time. Her mind was clearer, her heart lighter. She knew that tomorrow would bring new challenges, but she was ready to face them head-on.

With a smile, she turned off the light and crawled into bed, grateful for her journey.

# Chapter 3: Letting Go

Emily stood in the middle of her living room, surrounded by piles of items she had accumulated over the years. Books she had never read, kitchen gadgets she never used, and souvenirs from trips that seemed like a lifetime ago. Each item had a story, a reason for being, and a memory attached. The thought of letting go filled her with a strange mix of fear and excitement.

"Where do I even start?" Emily muttered to herself, feeling overwhelmed. She knew this was the next step in her journey towards minimalism, but the process was more daunting than she had anticipated.

Taking a deep breath, she decided to start small. She grabbed a box labeled "sentimental items" and sat down on the floor. Inside were mementos from her college days: concert tickets, birthday cards from friends, a dried rose from her first boyfriend, and a stack of old photographs. She picked up a photo of herself with her college roommates, taken on the day of their graduation. The image brought back a flood of memories—nights spent studying, laughing over late-night pizza, and dreaming about the future.

As she stared at the photo, a wave of nostalgia washed over her. She realized that while she cherished those memories, she hadn't spoken to any of her roommates in years. Life had moved on, and so had they. Emily's grip tightened on the photo, torn between holding on to the past and embracing the present.

"What are you doing?" a voice broke through her thoughts. Emily looked up to see Aaron standing in the doorway, a curious expression on his face.

Aaron had become a mentor of sorts to Emily. She had met him at a local minimalist meet-up a few weeks ago, and his calm, centered approach to life had drawn her in. He had been living as a minimalist for over a decade, and his home reflected his philosophy—simple, clean, and intentional. He had offered to help Emily on her journey, and she was grateful for his guidance.

"I'm... trying to let go," Emily replied, her voice tinged with uncertainty.

Aaron nodded and walked over, sitting down beside her. He glanced at the photo in her hand and smiled. "That's a great memory," he said. "But remember, it's just a memory. The photo isn't the memory itself."

Emily looked at him, confused. "What do you mean?"

Aaron leaned back, resting his hands on the floor behind him. "I mean that holding onto physical items because of the memories they carry can be a form of attachment. Those memories will always be with you, whether you have the photo or not. Letting go of the item doesn't mean letting go of the memory."

Emily thought about his words. She knew he was right, but it was easier said than done. She looked around her living room, at the piles of things that represented different chapters of her life. It felt like she was saying goodbye to a part of herself.

"I know it's hard," Aaron continued, sensing her hesitation. "But think about why you're doing this. You want to create space for new experiences, new memories. Holding onto the past can sometimes prevent us from moving forward."

Emily nodded slowly. She knew he was right. She wanted to embrace this new chapter of her life, free from the weight of material possessions. She took a deep breath and placed the photo in a pile of things to be donated. It was a small step, but it felt like a giant leap.

They continued going through the box together, item by item. Aaron helped Emily see each object for what it was—a physical representation of a memory, not the memory itself. As they worked, Emily began to feel lighter, as if a burden she hadn't even realized she was carrying was slowly being lifted.

After a few hours, they had sorted through several boxes, and Emily's living room was noticeably emptier. She looked around, feeling a sense of accomplishment. But as she glanced at the pile of items to be donated, a pang of anxiety hit her.

"What if I regret this?" she asked, her voice barely above a whisper.

Aaron smiled reassuringly. "It's normal to feel that way. Letting go can be scary because it forces us to confront the idea of impermanence. But remember, this isn't about deprivation. It's about making room for what truly matters to you."

Emily nodded, trying to absorb his words. She knew he was right, but the fear of loss was still there, lurking in the back of her mind. She took another deep breath and stood up, determined to keep going.

"Okay," she said, her voice steadier. "Let's keep going."

They moved on to the next box, labeled "childhood memories." Inside were toys, stuffed animals, and school projects Emily had kept for years. She picked up a faded stuffed bear, its fur worn from years of cuddling. It had been her favorite toy as a child, a source of comfort and security.

Holding the bear in her hands, Emily felt a lump form in her throat. It was just a toy, but it represented so much more—her childhood, her innocence, a time when life was simpler and carefree. She looked at Aaron, unsure of what to do.

"What does this bear mean to you?" Aaron asked gently.

Emily hesitated, trying to find the words. "It was my favorite toy as a kid. I used to take it everywhere with me. It... it made me feel safe."

Aaron nodded, understanding. "And does it still make you feel safe?"

Emily looked at the bear, then back at Aaron. "Not really," she admitted. "I mean, I don't need it anymore. I just... I don't know."

Aaron smiled. "It's okay. It's okay to let go. You're not losing the comfort it gave you as a child. You've just outgrown it. You have new sources of comfort and security now."

Emily considered his words. She thought about her life now—the friends she had, the career she was building, the new experiences she was embracing. She realized that she didn't need the bear anymore. It had served its purpose, and now it was time to let it go.

With a deep breath, she placed the bear in the donation pile. It wasn't easy, but it felt right. She was ready to move forward, to embrace a life of intentionality and purpose.

They continued sorting through the box, and as they did, Emily felt a sense of relief. Each item she let go of was like shedding a layer of her past, making room for a brighter, lighter future. She realized that letting go wasn't just about getting rid of things—it was about freeing herself from the weight of the past and embracing the present.

As the afternoon turned into evening, Emily and Aaron finished sorting through the last of the boxes. Emily's living room was almost unrecognizable—clean, open, and free from clutter. She looked around, feeling a sense of accomplishment and peace.

"I can't believe how much lighter I feel," she said, a smile spreading across her face.

Aaron nodded, smiling back. "That's the power of letting go. It's not just about getting rid of things. It's about creating space—space for new experiences, new opportunities, and a new way of living."

Emily nodded, feeling a newfound sense of clarity and purpose. She knew that this was just the beginning of her minimalist journey, but she was ready to embrace it fully. She was ready to let go of the past and make room for the future.

"Thank you, Aaron," she said, her voice filled with gratitude. "I couldn't have done this without you."

Aaron shook his head, smiling. "You did this, Emily. I just helped guide you. Remember, this is your journey. It's all about finding what works for you and what brings you joy."

Emily nodded, feeling a surge of determination. She knew she still had a long way to go, but she was ready to keep moving forward. She was ready to embrace the minimalist philosophy and live a life of intention and purpose.

As Aaron left, Emily stood in the doorway, watching him walk down the street. She felt a sense of peace she hadn't felt in years—a peace that came from knowing she was on the right path, a path that was true to herself.

Closing the door, she turned back to her living room, her heart full of hope and excitement. She knew there would be challenges ahead, but she was ready to face them. She was ready to let go, to embrace the present, and to live a life of simplicity and joy.

The Next Day

Emily woke up the next morning with a sense of lightness she hadn't felt in years. The sun was streaming through the windows, casting a warm glow over her newly decluttered living room. She stretched, feeling a newfound energy and excitement for the day ahead.

As she made her morning coffee, she thought about the day before—the boxes of items she had let go of, the memories she had confronted, and the peace she had found in the process. She realized that letting go wasn't just about getting rid of physical possessions. It was about releasing emotional baggage, letting go of the past, and making room for new experiences.

With her coffee in hand, Emily sat down at her kitchen table and opened her journal. She had started journaling as part of her minimalist journey, using it as a tool to reflect on her thoughts and feelings. Today, she felt inspired to write about her experience of letting go.

Dear Journal,

Yesterday was a big day. I let go of so many things—physical items, yes, but also memories, emotions, and a lot of fear. I didn't realize how much I had been holding onto, or how much it was weighing me down. It was hard to let go, but it was also incredibly freeing. I feel lighter today, more at peace. I'm excited for what's to come, and I'm ready to embrace this new chapter of my life.

I know there will be more challenges ahead, more things to let go of, but I'm ready. I'm ready to keep moving forward, to live with intention, and to find joy in the simple things.

Here's to a new beginning.

Emily closed her journal, feeling a sense of contentment. She knew she still had a lot to learn and a long way to go, but she was ready for the journey. She was ready to let go of the past and embrace the future with open arms.

Later That Week

As the week went on, Emily continued to declutter her apartment, tackling different areas each day. She went through her kitchen, letting go of gadgets and appliances she never used. She sorted through her bathroom, discarding old cosmetics and products that had expired. She even tackled her bookshelf, donating books she knew she would never read again.

With each item she let go of, Emily felt a little lighter, a little freer. She realized that she didn't need all these things to be happy. In fact, the more she let go, the more joy she found in the simplicity of her new lifestyle.

One evening, as she was sorting through a box of old letters and cards, Emily came across a letter from her grandmother. Her grandmother had passed away a few years ago, and the letter brought back a flood of memories. She remembered how her grandmother had always encouraged her to live a life of purpose and intention, to focus on what truly mattered.

Tears welled up in Emily's eyes as she read the letter, her grandmother's words resonating with her now more than ever.

"Dear Emily,

Life is short, and it's important to make the most of it. Don't get caught up in the material things. Focus on what truly matters—your relationships, your passions, your purpose. Live with intention, and find joy in the simple things. That's the key to a happy life.

Love, Grandma."

Emily wiped away her tears, feeling a sense of comfort and clarity. Her grandmother's words were a reminder of why she had started this journey in the first place. She wanted to live a life of purpose, to focus on what truly mattered, and to find joy in the simple things.

With a deep breath, Emily folded the letter and placed it in a special box, one she had set aside for items that truly brought her joy. She realized that it wasn't about getting rid of everything—it was about keeping what truly mattered and letting go of the rest.

A New Perspective

As Emily continued her minimalist journey, she began to notice a shift in her perspective. She started to see the world through a different lens, one that was focused on experiences rather than possessions, on quality rather than quantity.

She found herself enjoying the simple things more—taking a walk in the park, cooking a homemade meal, spending time with friends and family. She realized that happiness wasn't found in things, but in moments, in connections, and in living a life true to herself.

One evening, Emily met Aaron for coffee, eager to share her progress. As they sat down at a cozy café, she felt a sense of excitement and pride in how far she had come.

"I've been letting go of so much," she said, her eyes shining with enthusiasm. "I've decluttered my apartment, my mind, and my life. I feel so much lighter, so much freer. I can't believe how much has changed in just a few weeks."

Aaron smiled, nodding in approval. "That's amazing, Emily. I'm so proud of you. It sounds like you're embracing the minimalist philosophy."

Emily nodded, feeling a sense of accomplishment. "I am. I'm starting to realize that it's not just about getting rid of things. It's about living with intention, focusing on what truly matters, and finding joy in the simple things. It's about letting go of the past and making room for the future."

Aaron raised his coffee cup in a toast. "To letting go," he said, smiling.

Emily clinked her cup against his, feeling a surge of gratitude and joy. "To letting go," she echoed.

# Chapter 4: Digital Declutter

Emily sat at her kitchen table, sipping a cup of herbal tea as the morning sun streamed through the window. The past few weeks had been a whirlwind of transformation. She had started her minimalist journey by decluttering her wardrobe and letting go of sentimental items, and each small act of letting go had left her feeling lighter and more in control of her life.

Yet, despite the progress, there was still a lingering sense of unease. Her physical space was becoming more streamlined, but Emily couldn't shake the feeling that something else was weighing her down.

Her laptop sat open in front of her, its screen filled with a sea of notifications and unread emails. It was then that Emily realized where the weight was coming from: her digital life.

She had spent so much time focusing on decluttering her physical belongings that she hadn't considered the clutter that existed in her digital world. Emails, social media, apps, photos—everything had accumulated into a chaotic mess that constantly demanded her attention. Every time she opened her phone or laptop, she was bombarded with notifications, messages, and reminders of tasks she had yet to complete.

Determined to tackle this new challenge, Emily decided to start with her email. She opened her inbox and was greeted by over 5,000 unread messages. Most of them were promotional emails, newsletters she had never read, and outdated messages from years ago.

"Where do I even start?" she muttered to herself, feeling overwhelmed by the sheer volume of messages.

She remembered something Aaron had said at the minimalist meet-up: "Minimalism isn't just about physical clutter. It's about removing anything that doesn't add value to your life." With this in mind, Emily decided to approach her email with the same mindset she had applied to her wardrobe. She would keep only what was necessary and valuable, and discard the rest.

Step 1: The Purge

Emily took a deep breath and began by selecting all the promotional emails she had accumulated over the years. She hovered over the "delete" button, hesitating for a moment. What if she missed out on a sale or an important update?

"No," she told herself firmly. "This is about freedom, not fear." With a decisive click, she deleted over 3,000 emails in one go.

The sight of her newly cleared inbox gave her a surge of satisfaction, but she knew there was more work to be done. Next, she tackled the newsletters. She had subscribed to countless ones over the years, but rarely took the time to read them. She opened each one, assessing whether it still provided value or interest. For most, the answer was no.

Unsubscribing from each newsletter felt like breaking free from invisible chains that had tied her down. With each unsubscribe, she felt a small weight lift from her shoulders. By the end of the hour, Emily's inbox had been reduced to just a few hundred emails—mostly important work messages and personal correspondence she wanted to keep.

Step 2: Organizing What's Left

With her inbox now manageable, Emily decided to create folders to better organize the remaining emails. She made separate folders for work, personal, receipts, and important documents. This way, she could easily find what she needed without having to scroll through a cluttered inbox.

She moved all her work emails into the "Work" folder, which immediately made her inbox look cleaner. Personal emails went into their folder, and any important documents or receipts were filed away accordingly.

As she organized, Emily found a few emails from old friends she hadn't spoken to in years. She paused, taking a moment to read through them, smiling at the memories they brought back. She decided to keep these emails, not out of a sense of nostalgia, but because they reminded her of connections she wanted to rekindle.

By the time she finished organizing her inbox, Emily felt a sense of accomplishment. What had once been a source of stress and overwhelm was now a streamlined, manageable space.

Step 3: Tackling Digital Files

Next on Emily's list were the countless files cluttering her desktop and documents folder. She opened her desktop, staring at the maze of icons and random files that had accumulated over the years.

"Why do I have so many screenshots?" she wondered aloud, scrolling through a long list of unnamed image files. Most were pointless—screenshots of conversations, temporary downloads, and images she had saved for reasons she couldn't even remember.

She started by creating a folder labeled "Desktop Declutter" and began dragging all the unnecessary files into it. Her desktop slowly began to clear, and soon she was left with just a few essential icons. She then moved on to her documents folder, where she found even more chaos—old school papers, half-finished projects, and multiple versions of the same document.

Emily knew she needed a system, so she created new folders to categorize her files—"Personal," "Work," "Finance," and "Miscellaneous." She started sorting through her documents, discarding what was no longer needed and organizing what was left into the appropriate folders.

As she went through her files, she found herself feeling nostalgic over old photos and documents from her college days. At first, she felt tempted to keep everything, but she reminded herself of the principles of minimalism. Did these files add value to her current life? Did they serve a purpose or bring her joy?

Emily decided to keep a few key documents and photos that truly mattered to her, but the rest were deleted. She knew that memories didn't reside in the digital clutter but in her mind and heart.

Step 4: Streamlining Apps and Software

Feeling energized by her progress, Emily turned her attention to her phone. It had become an extension of herself, always within reach and constantly demanding her attention with notifications. She unlocked her phone and scrolled through pages of apps, many of which she hadn't used in months, if not years.

She decided to apply the same strategy as with her emails: assess each app and delete those that no longer served a purpose or added value.

First, she tackled social media. Emily had accounts on almost every platform but found that she rarely used most of them. She had been holding onto them out of fear of missing out, but now, she realized they were more of a distraction than a benefit. She deleted the apps she no longer used, keeping only one or two that she felt truly connected her with friends and family.

Next, she moved on to games and entertainment apps. Many were downloaded in moments of boredom but never used afterward. She deleted them without hesitation, clearing up valuable storage space.

Finally, Emily reviewed her productivity apps. She realized she had multiple apps for the same purpose—three different to-do list apps, two calendar apps, and several note-taking apps. She decided to consolidate, keeping only the ones she used most frequently and found the most effective.

As she deleted the unnecessary apps, Emily felt a growing sense of relief. Her phone screen became less cluttered, and she found herself breathing easier, no longer feeling overwhelmed by the sheer number of icons staring back at her.

Step 5: Managing Social Media and Notifications

With her phone decluttered, Emily decided it was time to address her social media habits. She had never been a heavy user, but she found herself mindlessly scrolling through her feeds more often than she cared to admit.

She opened her settings and turned off all non-essential notifications. No more pings and buzzes for likes, comments, or follows. She also set limits on her social media usage, deciding to check her accounts only once in the morning and once in the evening.

Emily knew she needed to be more intentional about how she used social media. Instead of letting it control her, she wanted to use it as a tool to connect with others and share meaningful experiences. She unfollowed accounts that didn't bring her joy or inspiration and focused on curating a feed that reflected her values and interests.

Step 6: Backing Up and Protecting What Matters

As Emily continued her digital declutter, she realized the importance of protecting her valuable digital assets. She had heard horror stories of people losing all their files due to a computer crash or stolen phone, and she didn't want to risk losing her own important documents and photos.

She invested in an external hard drive and began backing up all her important files, organizing them by category for easy access. She also set up a cloud storage account for additional security, ensuring that she could access her files from anywhere if needed.

Emily felt a sense of relief knowing that her digital life was now safe and secure. She had taken the necessary steps to protect what mattered and could now move forward without the fear of losing anything valuable.

Step 7: Establishing Digital Boundaries

The final step in Emily's digital declutter was establishing boundaries to prevent future digital clutter. She knew that if she didn't set rules for herself, she could easily fall back into old habits.

She created a digital declutter routine, setting aside time each month to go through her emails, files, and apps, deleting anything unnecessary and organizing what remained. She also set a rule to limit her screen time in the evenings, choosing to read a book or meditate instead of scrolling through her phone before bed.

With these boundaries in place, Emily felt confident that she could maintain a clutter-free digital life. She knew that minimalism wasn't a one-time event but an ongoing practice that required intention and mindfulness.

Reflection: The Mental Weight of Digital Clutter

As Emily sat back and reflected on her digital declutter journey, she realized just how much her digital life had been affecting her mental health. The constant notifications, overwhelming inbox, and chaotic files had created a sense of anxiety and stress that she hadn't fully acknowledged until now.

By decluttering her digital life, Emily felt a renewed sense of clarity and focus. She was no longer weighed down by the constant demands of her devices and could instead focus on what truly mattered to her. She had created a digital space that was intentional and aligned with her minimalist values.

Emily knew that there would be challenges ahead and that maintaining a minimalist lifestyle would require ongoing effort and mindfulness. But she felt ready to face those challenges, armed with the knowledge and tools she had gained from her digital declutter experience.

As she closed her laptop and put her phone away, Emily felt a sense of peace wash over her. She had taken control of her digital life, and in doing so, she had taken another step toward living a life of simplicity, purpose, and fulfillment.

# Chapter 5: The Minimalist Mindset

Emily sat at her kitchen table, staring at the blank page in her journal. She had spent the past few weeks decluttering her apartment, getting rid of clothes, trinkets, and even some furniture. The physical transformation of her space was undeniable. Yet, despite the cleaner, more organized surroundings, she felt a persistent restlessness within.

Earlier that morning, Aaron had texted her, asking if she wanted to grab coffee and talk about the next steps in her minimalist journey. "Sure, why not?" she had replied, though she wasn't sure what else there could be to learn. She had purged her belongings, organized her digital files, and even started saying no to unnecessary commitments. What more could minimalism offer?

Emily's phone buzzed, snapping her back to reality. It was Aaron again, reminding her of their meeting time. She closed her journal, grabbed her bag, and headed out the door, still pondering what the day might bring.

The coffee shop was nestled on a quiet corner of a bustling neighborhood, a small oasis amid the city's chaos. Aaron was already there, sitting by the window with a mug of tea and a notebook. He waved as Emily walked in, motioning for her to join him.

"Hey, Emily," Aaron greeted with a warm smile. "How's everything going with your decluttering?"

"It's been... interesting," Emily replied, taking a seat across from him. "I mean, I've gotten rid of a lot of stuff, but I still feel like something's missing. Or maybe something's not quite clicking yet."

Aaron nodded, as if he had expected this. "That's completely normal. Physical decluttering is just the first step. Minimalism isn't just about getting rid of things; it's about transforming the way you think and approach life. It's about adopting a minimalist mindset."

Emily frowned slightly. "What do you mean by that?"

Aaron took a sip of his tea, gathering his thoughts. "A minimalist mindset is about living with intention and focus. It's about understanding what truly matters to you and aligning your actions with those values. Minimalism is as much a mental and emotional practice as it is a physical one."

Emily thought about this for a moment. "I guess I've been so focused on the decluttering part that I haven't really thought about the mental side of things."

"That's understandable," Aaron said. "Most people start with the tangible because it's easier to see the results. But the real transformation happens when you start changing your mindset. It's about asking yourself why you're holding on to certain things, why you're doing certain activities, and whether they actually bring you joy or value."

Emily nodded slowly, taking in his words. "So, how do I start developing this mindset?"

Aaron smiled. "Let's start with a simple exercise. I want you to think about what's truly important to you. What are your core values? What do you want your life to look like?"

Emily hesitated. These were questions she had never really asked herself before. She had always been so busy trying to keep up with work, friends, and the latest trends that she hadn't stopped to consider what she actually wanted.

"I'm not sure," she admitted. "I mean, I want to be happy, of course. And successful. But beyond that, I'm not really sure."

Aaron nodded, not at all surprised. "That's okay. It takes time to figure these things out. Why don't you try writing down some thoughts in your journal? Start by listing the things that make you feel fulfilled or content, and the things that drain your energy or make you unhappy."

Emily pulled out her journal and began to write. She listed things like spending time with her family, reading, hiking, and working on creative projects. On the other side, she noted the constant pressure of work, social media, and trying to keep up with the latest trends.

As she wrote, she felt a sense of clarity emerging. She realized that many of the things she had been spending her time and energy on were not aligned with what truly mattered to her.

Aaron watched as she wrote, giving her space to explore her thoughts. After a few minutes, he spoke up. "How does that feel?"

Emily looked up from her journal, a thoughtful expression on her face. "It feels... enlightening, I guess. I'm starting to see that a lot of the things I've been focused on don't actually make me happy."

"Exactly," Aaron said, leaning forward. "The minimalist mindset is about recognizing what adds value to your life and letting go of the rest. It's about being intentional with your time, energy, and resources."

Emily nodded. "I like the sound of that. But how do I actually put it into practice?"

Aaron smiled. "It starts with mindfulness. Being present in the moment and aware of your thoughts, feelings, and actions. It's about making conscious choices instead of just going through the motions."

He paused for a moment, letting his words sink in. "For example, before you make a purchase, ask yourself if you really need it or if it will genuinely add value to your life. Before you say yes to a commitment, consider whether it aligns with your values and if it's something you actually want to do."

Emily nodded, thinking back to all the times she had bought something on impulse or agreed to plans she wasn't excited about just to please others.

"It's also about simplifying your mental space," Aaron continued. "This means letting go of negative thoughts, limiting beliefs, and emotional baggage that no longer serve you. It's about cultivating a positive mindset and focusing on gratitude and abundance rather than scarcity and lack."

Emily listened intently, feeling inspired by Aaron's words. She realized that minimalism wasn't just about getting rid of physical stuff; it was about creating space in her mind and life for what truly mattered.

"That makes a lot of sense," she said. "But it sounds easier said than done."

Aaron chuckled. "It definitely takes practice. It's not something that happens overnight. But the more you practice mindfulness and intentionality, the more natural it becomes."

He leaned back in his chair, a thoughtful expression on his face. "One of the things that helped me was adopting a daily mindfulness practice. It can be something as simple as taking a few minutes each day to meditate, journal, or just sit in silence and reflect. It's about creating a habit of checking in with yourself and staying connected to your inner self."

Emily liked the sound of that. She had always been interested in mindfulness and meditation but had never really taken the time to practice it.

"I think I'd like to try that," she said. "Do you have any tips on how to get started?"

Aaron nodded. "Absolutely. Start small. Just five minutes a day to begin with. Find a quiet space, close your eyes, and focus on your breath. If your mind starts to wander, gently bring it back to your breath. The goal isn't to stop your thoughts but to become aware of them and let them pass without attachment."

Emily took out her notebook and jotted down Aaron's advice. She felt a sense of excitement, eager to start this new practice and see how it could help her develop a minimalist mindset.

Aaron glanced at his watch. "I should probably get going, but I'm glad we had this chat. Remember, minimalism is a journey, not a destination. It's about continuous growth and learning. Don't be too hard on yourself. Take it one step at a time."

Emily nodded, feeling grateful for Aaron's guidance and support. "Thanks, Aaron. I really appreciate it."

"Anytime," Aaron replied with a warm smile. "I'm always here if you need to talk or have any questions. Just remember, the minimalist mindset is about living with intention and focus. It's about creating a life that reflects your true values and priorities."

As Emily left the coffee shop, she felt a renewed sense of purpose. She was excited to start exploring the mental and emotional aspects of minimalism and to continue her journey toward a simpler, more intentional life.

Back at home, Emily set up a small corner in her bedroom as her mindfulness space. She laid out a soft cushion on the floor, placed a small candle on the windowsill, and set her journal nearby. She sat down, crossed her legs, and closed her eyes, taking a deep breath to center herself.

For the next five minutes, she focused on her breath, feeling the rise and fall of her chest with each inhale and exhale. Her mind wandered several times, but she gently brought it back to her breath each time, just as Aaron had suggested.

When the timer on her phone went off, she opened her eyes and took a deep breath. She felt a sense of calm and clarity that she hadn't experienced in a long time. It was a small step, but it was a start.

Over the next few days, Emily continued to practice mindfulness daily. She found that the simple act of sitting in silence and focusing on her breath helped her feel more grounded and centered. She also started to notice when her mind was cluttered with negative thoughts or when she was feeling overwhelmed.

One evening, after a particularly stressful day at work, Emily decided to try a different mindfulness exercise. She took out her journal and wrote down all the things that were bothering her, getting them out of her head and onto paper. Then, she made a list of things she was grateful for, focusing on the positive aspects of her life.

As she wrote, she felt a shift in her mindset. She realized that even though her day had been stressful, there were still many things to be grateful for. She felt a sense of peace and contentment, knowing that she had the power to choose her thoughts and focus on the positive.

Emily continued to explore different mindfulness practices, from guided meditations to mindful walking and even mindful eating. She found that each practice helped her become more aware of her thoughts and feelings and more intentional in her actions.

As the weeks went by, Emily noticed a subtle but profound change in her mindset. She felt less stressed and more at peace with herself. She was more mindful of her choices and more intentional in her actions. She found herself saying no to things that didn't align with her values and yes to things that brought her joy and fulfillment.

She also noticed a shift in her relationships. She was more present with her friends and family, truly listening and engaging in conversations rather than being distracted by her phone or her thoughts. She found that her relationships became deeper and more meaningful as a result.

One day, while walking through a park near her apartment, Emily reflected on how much her life had changed since she started her minimalist journey. She felt a sense of gratitude for the path she had chosen and the lessons she had learned along the way.

She realized that minimalism wasn't just about having less but about living more. It was about creating space in her life for what truly mattered, about being intentional with her time, energy, and resources.

As she sat on a bench, watching the leaves dance in the breeze, Emily felt a deep sense of peace and contentment. She knew that she still had a long way to go and that there would be challenges along the way, but she was excited to continue her journey and see where it would take her.

She took out her journal and wrote a simple affirmation: "I choose to live with intention, focus, and purpose. I am grateful for this journey and the person I am becoming."

# Chapter 6: Facing Consumer Culture

Emily stood at the entrance of the mall, her fingers tingling with a mixture of excitement and anxiety. She hadn't been here in weeks. Normally, she would have been ecstatic about a shopping trip, but today felt different. Today, she was acutely aware of the undercurrent pulling at her — the lure of consumer culture and the contradiction it posed to her new minimalist journey.

She had agreed to meet her friends Sarah and Jess for a girls' day out. They had planned lunch, a movie, and, of course, shopping. It was a ritual they had indulged in for years, a way to bond over shared tastes and the thrill of finding the perfect outfit. But as Emily stood there, staring at the polished floors and neon signs, she felt a knot form in her stomach. The familiar buzz of the mall, the scent of cinnamon pretzels wafting through the air, the bright displays pulling shoppers in — all of it felt different now. She could see the trap laid out for her and the thousands of other shoppers who would walk through these doors today.

"There you are!" Sarah's voice cut through Emily's thoughts. She turned to see her friends walking toward her, bags already in hand. They were chatting excitedly, their faces lit up with the joy of the hunt. Jess, a brunette with an eye for style, had already snagged a new pair of boots. Sarah, ever the deal hunter, was holding up a dress she had scored for half off.

"Em, you're not gonna believe the sale they're having at Zara!" Sarah exclaimed, grabbing Emily's arm. "Come on, you have to check it out."

Emily hesitated. She had vowed to stick to her minimalist principles, to resist the urge to buy things she didn't need. But the excitement in Sarah's eyes was infectious, and before she knew it, she was being dragged through the mall, past glittering displays and sleek mannequins, into the heart of the shopping frenzy.

The store was packed, a sea of people rifling through racks and stacks of clothes. Emily's senses were assaulted by the mix of perfumes, the hum of chatter, and the blaring pop music. She felt herself being swept up in the current of it all, her heart racing as she moved from rack to rack. Every corner she turned revealed a new temptation: a stylish blazer, a cozy sweater, a pair of jeans that promised the perfect fit. Her fingers brushed against soft fabrics, and she felt the familiar thrill of possibility — of finding something new, something that would make her feel good.

But as she stood there, holding a silk blouse up to the light, a voice in her head cut through the noise. What are you doing? You don't need this. You came here to spend time with your friends, not to buy more stuff.

Emily put the blouse back on the rack, her hands trembling slightly. She looked around, noticing the expressions on the faces of the shoppers around her. Some looked happy, but many had a look of determination, of almost desperation. It was as if they were on a mission, hunting for something to fill a void they couldn't quite name. She saw herself in them — the endless chase, the temporary high of a new purchase, followed by the inevitable crash of dissatisfaction.

She took a deep breath, trying to steady herself. She knew what she had to do. "Hey, Sarah, Jess," she called out, raising her voice over the music. "I think I'm going to step outside for a bit. I just need some air."

Sarah and Jess exchanged a puzzled glance. "Are you okay?" Jess asked, concern flickering across her face.

"Yeah, I'm fine," Emily said, forcing a smile. "I just need a moment. I'll meet you guys in the food court?"

Sarah nodded, giving Emily's arm a reassuring squeeze. "Sure thing, Em. We'll see you in a bit."

Emily hurried out of the store, her heart still pounding. She pushed through the throngs of shoppers and made her way to the nearest exit. The fresh air hit her like a wave, and she inhaled deeply, trying to clear her head. She walked over to a bench and sat down, closing her eyes for a moment.

The mall loomed behind her, a gleaming temple of consumerism, and she felt a pang of guilt. How could she have been so easily swayed? She thought she was stronger than this, more committed to her new path. But the pull of old habits, of comfort in the familiar, was stronger than she had anticipated.

She reached into her bag and pulled out her phone, scrolling through her contacts until she found Aaron's number. Her finger hovered over the call button for a moment before she pressed it. Aaron had become her mentor, guiding her through the early stages of her minimalist journey. He always knew what to say to keep her grounded.

"Hey, Emily," Aaron's voice came through, warm and calm as ever. "What's up?"

"Hey, Aaron," she said, trying to steady her voice. "I just... I needed to talk to someone. I'm at the mall with my friends, and I almost bought something. I feel like I'm failing at this whole minimalism thing."

There was a pause on the other end of the line, and Emily could almost hear Aaron's thoughtful smile. "It's okay, Emily," he said gently. "You're not failing. This is part of the process. Temptation is everywhere, especially in a place like a mall. The fact that you recognized it and walked away is a huge step."

Emily sighed, running a hand through her hair. "I just felt so overwhelmed. It's like everything here is designed to make you want more, to make you feel like you need more to be happy."

Aaron chuckled softly. "That's because it is. The whole consumer culture is built on the idea that happiness can be bought, that there's always something new you need. But remember, minimalism isn't about denying yourself; it's about being intentional with your choices. It's okay to feel tempted. What matters is what you do with that feeling."

Emily nodded, feeling a bit of the tension ease from her shoulders. "I guess you're right. It's just... hard, you know?"

"I know," Aaron said. "But you're doing great, Emily. It takes time to rewire those habits, to change the way you think about things. Be kind to yourself. You've already made so much progress."

Emily smiled, a sense of calm washing over her. "Thanks, Aaron. I needed to hear that."

"Anytime," he replied. "Now go enjoy your time with your friends. Remember, minimalism is about focusing on what truly matters. And today, that's spending time with people you care about."

Emily hung up, slipping her phone back into her bag. She took a few more deep breaths, feeling the warmth of the sun on her face. She could do this. She could enjoy the day without getting caught up in the frenzy of buying things she didn't need.

With renewed resolve, she headed back into the mall, weaving through the crowds until she found Sarah and Jess in the food court. They were sitting at a table, sipping on iced coffees and chatting animatedly.

"Hey, there you are!" Jess exclaimed as Emily approached. "Feeling better?"

"Yeah," Emily said, sliding into a chair. "Thanks for understanding. I just needed a moment."

"Of course," Sarah said, reaching across the table to squeeze Emily's hand. "We've all been there."

They spent the next hour catching up, laughing about old memories and sharing stories from their lives. Emily felt a sense of contentment settle over her. This was what mattered — not the stuff they bought or the clothes they wore, but the connections they shared, the moments of joy and laughter.

As they finished their coffees, Jess suggested they check out a new bookstore that had opened on the other side of the mall. Emily hesitated for a moment, but then she smiled. A bookstore she could handle. Books, to her, were a source of knowledge and inspiration, not clutter.

They made their way to the store, a cozy little shop with shelves lined with books of every genre. The smell of fresh paper and ink filled the air, and Emily felt a wave of nostalgia wash over her. She had always loved books, had always found solace in their pages.

As her friends browsed, Emily wandered over to a section on mindfulness and simplicity. Her eyes fell on a book titled "The Joy of Less: A Minimalist Guide to Decluttering, Organizing, and Simplifying." She pulled it off the shelf, flipping through the pages. The author wrote about the freedom of letting go, the peace that came from living with less. Emily felt a connection to the words, a reminder of why she had started this journey in the first place.

She made her way to the counter, purchasing the book with a sense of purpose. This was a purchase that aligned with her values, one that would help her on her path. As she rejoined her friends, she felt a renewed sense of clarity. She didn't need to give up shopping altogether; she just needed to be mindful of what she bought, to ensure it added value to her life rather than clutter.

They spent the rest of the afternoon exploring the mall, but this time, Emily felt no urge to buy. She admired the window displays, tried on a few things for fun, but always with the understanding that she didn't need any of it. She was content with what she had, with who she was becoming.

As the day came to a close, they made their way back to the parking lot, the sun setting in a blaze of orange and pink. Emily felt a sense of peace settle over her. She had faced the temptations of consumer culture and had come out stronger. She knew there would be more challenges ahead, but she also knew she was on the right path.

"Thanks for a great day, guys," she said, giving Sarah and Jess each a hug. "I had a lot of fun."

"Me too," Jess said, smiling. "We should do this more often."

"Definitely," Sarah agreed. "But maybe next time, we can skip the shopping and just hang out somewhere quiet. Like a park or something."

Emily grinned, feeling a warm glow in her chest. "That sounds perfect."

As she drove home, Emily reflected on the day, on the lessons she had learned. Minimalism wasn't about depriving herself or rejecting her past. It was about making conscious choices, about focusing on what truly mattered. And today, she had done just that.

When she got home, she placed her new book on the coffee table, feeling a sense of accomplishment. She had faced the pull of consumer culture and had chosen a different path, one that led to fulfillment and peace. She knew it wouldn't always be easy, but she was ready for the journey ahead.

She made herself a cup of tea and sat down on the couch, opening the book to the first page. As she began to read, she felt a sense of calm wash over her. This was what she had been searching for — not in the aisles of a store, but within herself.

And for the first time in a long time, she felt truly free.

# Chapter 7: Minimalist Relationships

Emily sat at her favorite café, the comforting aroma of freshly brewed coffee surrounding her. She sipped her latte thoughtfully, staring out the window at the bustling street outside. The city was alive with people, yet she felt oddly disconnected. Her phone buzzed with a new message from Claire, an old college friend she hadn't spoken to in months. They had been close once, but as the years passed, their lives had diverged significantly. Claire was married with two kids, living in the suburbs, while Emily was still single and navigating the maze of city life.

She glanced at the message:

Claire: "Hey! It's been so long. Let's catch up soon. How about lunch this weekend?"

Emily smiled at the invitation, but a familiar unease settled in. Lunch with Claire often meant a barrage of questions about why Emily wasn't married yet, why she hadn't moved out of the city, and why she hadn't yet found a 'real' career. It wasn't that she didn't love Claire—she did. But their conversations always left her feeling judged and misunderstood.

Emily's journey into minimalism had made her acutely aware of the value of her time and energy. She had learned to let go of physical possessions that no longer served her, but the next step, as Aaron had pointed out during one of their many conversations, was to evaluate her relationships.

"You need to surround yourself with people who lift you up, who understand your journey," Aaron had said, his eyes earnest. "Minimalism isn't just about things, it's about connections too."

Emily had nodded, thinking of all the people in her life who left her feeling drained or unfulfilled. She had always been a people-pleaser, going out of her way to maintain friendships even when they no longer brought her joy. It was time for that to change.

Emily responded to Claire's message:

Emily: "Hi Claire! Great to hear from you. I'm pretty swamped this weekend, but let's find another time to catch up. Hope all is well with you and the family!"

She hit send, feeling a mix of relief and guilt. She didn't want to cut Claire out of her life, but she needed to protect her energy. Claire was someone from her past who might not fit into her future—at least, not in the same way she once had.

Emily put her phone away and focused on the present moment, listening to the chatter of the café and the soft hum of the espresso machine. She was trying to practice mindfulness, something Aaron had introduced her to. It helped her feel grounded and connected to the here and now, rather than being caught up in past regrets or future anxieties.

As she sat there, she thought about the relationships that did bring her joy. She thought of Sarah, a new friend she had met at a minimalist workshop. They had hit it off immediately, bonding over their shared love of simple living and meaningful conversations. Sarah was someone who understood her journey and encouraged her to stay true to herself.

Emily made a mental note to reach out to Sarah. She wanted to nurture that friendship, to invest in connections that were aligned with her values.

Suddenly, her phone buzzed again, pulling her out of her thoughts. It was a text from Megan, her roommate.

Megan: "Hey! Are you coming home soon? We need to talk."

Emily frowned. Megan's texts were usually light-hearted, filled with jokes or memes. A 'we need to talk' message was out of character. She quickly paid for her coffee and headed home, her mind racing with possibilities.

When Emily opened the door to their apartment, she found Megan sitting on the couch, her face serious.

"Hey, what's up?" Emily asked, trying to sound casual as she hung up her coat.

Megan looked up, her expression softening slightly. "Emily, we need to talk about something important."

Emily's heart pounded. She had a feeling she knew where this was going. Over the past few months, her journey into minimalism had caused some tension between them. Emily's desire to declutter the apartment and simplify her lifestyle had clashed with Megan's love for shopping and keeping up with trends.

"Is this about the minimalism thing again?" Emily asked, sitting down across from Megan.

Megan sighed, running a hand through her hair. "Yeah, it is. I know you're really into this whole minimalist lifestyle, and I respect that. But I feel like it's affecting our living situation. You keep wanting to get rid of things, and I feel like I'm walking on eggshells in my own home."

Emily felt a pang of guilt. She hadn't realized how much her actions were impacting Megan. "I'm sorry, Megan. I didn't mean to make you feel that way. I guess I've been so focused on my own journey that I didn't consider how it was affecting you."

Megan nodded, her eyes softening. "I appreciate that, Emily. I really do. I just think we need to find a balance. I want to support you, but I also want to feel comfortable in my own space."

Emily nodded, understanding. She realized that her minimalism journey was about finding balance, not imposing her lifestyle on others. "You're right, Megan. I want this to be a home for both of us. Maybe we can set some boundaries, like you have your space and I have mine, and we respect each other's choices."

Megan smiled, relief washing over her face. "I think that sounds like a good plan. I'm glad we talked about this."

Emily felt a weight lift off her shoulders. She realized that minimalism wasn't about having fewer things; it was about having more of what mattered. And what mattered most to her was maintaining a healthy, respectful relationship with her roommate.

Over the next few days, Emily spent a lot of time thinking about her relationships. She started to make a list of people who truly enriched her life, people who understood her and supported her journey. She also made a list of relationships that felt draining or one-sided. It was a tough exercise, but she knew it was necessary.

One of the names that came up on the latter list was Jessica, a friend from her corporate job. Jessica was fun and outgoing, but their conversations often revolved around gossip and superficial topics. Emily realized that she often felt exhausted after spending time with Jessica, drained by the negativity that seemed to surround her.

Then there was Jake, an old flame who would pop up occasionally with a late-night text or a casual invite for drinks. Their relationship had always been complicated, a rollercoaster of emotions and unfulfilled promises. Every time Emily saw his name on her phone, she felt a mix of excitement and dread. She knew that Jake wasn't good for her, but it was hard to let go of the idea of him.

Emily decided it was time to make some changes. She couldn't continue to hold on to relationships that no longer served her. She needed to create space for the connections that did.

She started with Jessica, sending a polite but firm message explaining that she needed to focus on her well-being and that she was taking a step back from certain social activities. It wasn't easy, and Emily felt a pang of guilt as she hit send, but she knew it was the right thing to do.

Next, she turned to Jake. Her heart pounded as she typed out the words she had been rehearsing in her mind for so long:

Emily: "Hey Jake, I've been doing a lot of thinking, and I've realized that I need to focus on myself and my own happiness. I don't think we're good for each other, and I need to let go of this. I hope you understand."

She hit send and put her phone down, her hands shaking. She felt a wave of emotion wash over her—sadness, relief, fear. She wasn't sure what the future held, but she knew she was taking a step in the right direction.

A few weeks passed, and Emily began to feel a sense of clarity and lightness she hadn't experienced in years. She had fewer social engagements, but the ones she did have were meaningful and fulfilling. She spent more time with Sarah, going on long walks in the park and having deep conversations over cups of herbal tea. She reconnected with an old friend from high school, Emma, who had recently moved to the city and was also exploring minimalism. Their friendship felt like a breath of fresh air, filled with honesty and mutual understanding.

Emily also made an effort to deepen her relationship with Aaron. They met up regularly for coffee or lunch, discussing everything from minimalism to philosophy to their hopes and dreams. Aaron was a constant source of support and inspiration, encouraging Emily to stay true to herself and her values.

One evening, as they sat in a quiet corner of a cozy café, Aaron turned to Emily with a thoughtful expression. "You know, Emily, I've been thinking a lot about relationships lately. I think minimalism is about quality over quantity, in every aspect of life."

Emily nodded, sipping her chamomile tea. "I've realized that too. It's not about having a lot of friends or acquaintances; it's about having meaningful connections that add value to your life."

Aaron smiled, his eyes warm. "Exactly. And it's okay to let go of relationships that no longer serve you. It doesn't mean you don't care about those people; it just means you're choosing to prioritize your well-being."

Emily nodded, feeling a sense of affirmation. "It's been hard, but I feel like I'm finally starting to understand what that means. I'm learning to let go of the guilt and focus on what truly matters."

Aaron reached across the table, giving her hand a reassuring squeeze. "You're doing great, Emily. Remember, this is a journey, not a destination. It's about finding what works for you and being okay with letting go of the rest."

Emily smiled, feeling a warmth spread through her chest. She was grateful for Aaron's friendship and for the support he had given her throughout her minimalist journey. She knew that she still had a lot to learn, but she was confident that she was on the right path.

As they left the café and walked down the quiet, moonlit street, Emily felt a sense of peace and contentment. She realized that minimalism wasn't just about decluttering her physical space; it was about decluttering her life, making room for the things—and the people—that truly mattered.

The next day, Emily woke up feeling refreshed and energized. She decided to spend the day focusing on herself, doing things that brought her joy and fulfillment. She started with a morning yoga session, stretching her body and calming her mind. She then prepared a simple, nourishing breakfast of avocado toast and fresh fruit, savoring each bite mindfully.

After breakfast, she took a walk to the local farmers' market, enjoying the crisp autumn air and the vibrant colors of the season. She picked up some fresh vegetables and flowers, feeling a deep appreciation for the simplicity and beauty of nature.

As she strolled through the market, she ran into Emma, who was also there picking up some groceries.

"Emily! What a pleasant surprise!" Emma exclaimed, her face lighting up with a smile.

"Emma! Great to see you!" Emily replied, giving her friend a warm hug.

They decided to grab a coffee and catch up, finding a quiet spot at a nearby café. Emily felt a sense of gratitude as she sat across from Emma, realizing how much she valued their friendship. Emma was someone who truly understood her journey, someone who didn't judge or criticize but supported and encouraged her.

They spent the next hour talking about everything from their minimalist experiences to their favorite books to their plans for the future. Emily felt a deep sense of connection, a feeling of being seen and heard.

As they parted ways, Emily felt a renewed sense of purpose. She knew that she still had a lot to learn and a lot of growth to do, but she was confident in the direction she was heading. She was building a life that was aligned with her values, a life that was simple, intentional, and full of meaning.

That evening, Emily decided to host a small gathering at her apartment. She invited a few close friends, including Sarah, Emma, and Aaron. She wanted to create an intimate, meaningful experience, focusing on quality over quantity.

As she prepared a simple, wholesome meal of roasted vegetables, quinoa salad, and homemade bread, Emily felt a sense of anticipation and excitement. She set the table with care, using her favorite ceramic plates and linen napkins, adding a few candles and a vase of fresh flowers to create a warm, inviting atmosphere.

When her friends arrived, the apartment was filled with laughter, conversation, and the delicious aroma of home-cooked food. They sat around the table, sharing stories and experiences, talking about their hopes, dreams, and challenges. Emily felt a deep sense of joy and fulfillment, surrounded by people who understood and supported her.

After dinner, they moved to the living room, sitting on the floor with cups of herbal tea. They talked late into the night, sharing their thoughts on minimalism, relationships, and life. Emily felt a sense of connection and belonging, knowing that she was building a community of like-minded individuals who shared her values and vision.

As the evening came to a close, Emily walked her friends to the door, hugging each of them warmly. She felt a deep sense of gratitude for the meaningful connections she had cultivated, for the people who had come into her life and enriched it in so many ways.

After everyone had left, Emily sat down on the couch, reflecting on the evening. She realized that minimalism wasn't just about having fewer things; it was about having more of what mattered. It was about creating space for the people and experiences that brought joy, fulfillment, and meaning to her life.

She smiled to herself, feeling a sense of peace and contentment. She knew that she still had a lot to learn, but she was confident in the path she was on. She was building a life that was true to herself, a life that was simple, intentional, and full of love.

Emily got up, turned off the lights, and headed to bed, feeling a deep sense of gratitude for the journey she was on.

# Chapter 8: Mindful Eating

Emily had always thought of herself as a healthy eater. Her fridge was stocked with organic vegetables, almond milk, and a variety of superfoods she'd read about in wellness magazines. But despite her best intentions, she often found herself reaching for convenience—takeout meals, sugary snacks, and quick fixes. Her relationship with food, much like her relationship with possessions, was complicated and laden with emotional baggage.

It was on a rainy Sunday afternoon, during one of her now-routine decluttering sessions, that Emily stumbled upon an old food journal. She flipped through its pages, filled with detailed accounts of meals, calorie counts, and obsessive notes about her diet. She remembered those days vividly, the endless cycle of restrictive eating, bingeing, and guilt.

The sight of it made her pause. She hadn't thought much about her eating habits since she began her minimalist journey. Her focus had been on her possessions, her digital life, and her relationships. But now, as she stood in her kitchen, she realized that her approach to food was just as cluttered as her closet had once been.

That evening, she decided to invite Aaron over for dinner. Over the past few months, Aaron had become not just a mentor but a friend. They had shared countless conversations about minimalism, life, and purpose, and she valued his insights. As she began preparing the meal, chopping vegetables and simmering a pot of quinoa, she couldn't help but think about her relationship with food.

When Aaron arrived, he brought with him a sense of calm and ease that Emily found refreshing. They sat down at her small, uncluttered dining table, and Emily served the meal—a simple stir-fry of vegetables and tofu, garnished with fresh herbs.

"This looks great," Aaron said, taking a deep breath and inhaling the aroma of the dish. "Thank you for inviting me over."

"I'm glad you could come," Emily replied, smiling. "I've been thinking a lot about my journey with minimalism, and I realized there's an area I haven't really tackled yet—food."

Aaron nodded thoughtfully as he took a bite of the stir-fry. "Mindful eating is a big part of minimalist living. It's not just about what we eat, but how we eat, and our relationship with food."

Emily's interest was piqued. "I've heard about mindful eating before, but I'm not sure I really understand it. Can you tell me more?"

Aaron set down his fork and took a sip of water. "Mindful eating is about being fully present when you eat. It's about paying attention to the flavors, textures, and aromas of your food, and really savoring each bite. It's also about listening to your body's hunger and fullness cues, rather than eating out of habit or emotion."

Emily thought about her own eating habits. She often ate while distracted—scrolling through her phone, watching TV, or working on her laptop. She rarely took the time to truly enjoy her food. "I think I've been eating mindlessly for a long time," she admitted. "I'm always in such a rush, and I use food as a way to cope with stress or boredom."

Aaron nodded. "Many of us do. But by becoming more mindful about our eating, we can transform our relationship with food. It's about making eating a nourishing and enjoyable experience, rather than just another task on our to-do list."

Over the next few days, Emily decided to experiment with mindful eating. She began by setting aside time for meals, free from distractions. She put her phone on silent, turned off the TV, and sat down at the table with a plate of food.

At first, it felt strange to eat without any distractions. She was used to multitasking, to eating quickly and without much thought. But as she took her first bite and focused on the taste and texture of the food, she noticed something she hadn't experienced in a long time—a sense of satisfaction and enjoyment.

She chewed slowly, savoring the flavors and appreciating the effort that went into preparing the meal. She realized how disconnected she had been from the experience of eating, how she had been rushing through meals without truly tasting or appreciating them.

As she continued to practice mindful eating, she began to notice the signals her body was sending her. She became more aware of her hunger and fullness cues, learning to eat when she was hungry and stop when she was satisfied. She realized that she often ate out of habit or emotion, rather than true physical hunger.

One evening, after a particularly stressful day at work, Emily found herself reaching for a bag of chips. She paused, recognizing the familiar urge to eat as a way to soothe her emotions. Instead of mindlessly eating, she took a deep breath and asked herself if she was truly hungry. The answer was no.

She decided to make herself a cup of herbal tea instead, and sat down with her journal to reflect on her feelings. She wrote about her stress and frustration, allowing herself to process her emotions without using food as a crutch. It was a small victory, but it felt significant.

As Emily continued to explore mindful eating, she began to simplify her meals. She focused on whole, unprocessed foods that were nourishing and satisfying. She discovered the joy of cooking with fresh ingredients, experimenting with new recipes and flavors.

She also started to pay attention to where her food came from, choosing local and sustainable options whenever possible. She realized that minimalism wasn't just about decluttering her possessions, but also about making conscious choices in all areas of her life, including the food she ate.

One weekend, Emily decided to visit a local farmers' market. She had read about the benefits of eating seasonal and locally-grown produce, and she wanted to support local farmers. As she wandered through the market, she was struck by the vibrant colors and aromas of the fresh fruits and vegetables.

She struck up a conversation with a farmer selling heirloom tomatoes. "These look amazing," she said, picking up a plump, red tomato and inhaling its sweet, earthy scent.

The farmer smiled. "Thank you. We grow them right here in town, using organic practices. There's nothing quite like a fresh, vine-ripened tomato."

Emily bought a few tomatoes, along with some leafy greens, fresh herbs, and a loaf of crusty bread. She felt a sense of connection to the food she was buying, knowing that it was grown with care and that she was supporting local agriculture.

Back at home, she made herself a simple lunch of sliced tomatoes on toast, drizzled with olive oil and sprinkled with sea salt and fresh basil. As she took her first bite, she closed her eyes and savored the explosion of flavors—the sweetness of the tomatoes, the richness of the olive oil, the hint of salt and pepper.

It was a simple meal, but it was one of the most delicious things she had ever tasted. She realized that food didn't have to be complicated or fancy to be enjoyable. Sometimes, the simplest meals were the most satisfying.

As weeks went by, Emily noticed other changes in her relationship with food. She began to feel more in tune with her body, more aware of how different foods made her feel. She noticed that she had more energy and felt less bloated when she ate whole, unprocessed foods. She also found that she didn't crave sugary snacks or junk food as much as she used to.

She started to view food not just as fuel, but as nourishment for both her body and soul. She appreciated the process of preparing and cooking meals, finding joy in the ritual of chopping vegetables, stirring pots, and plating dishes. She realized that eating was not just about filling her stomach, but about nourishing her body, mind, and spirit.

One evening, as Emily was preparing dinner, she decided to try something new. She had recently read about the practice of gratitude, and she wanted to incorporate it into her mindful eating routine. She sat down at the table, her plate filled with a colorful array of roasted vegetables and quinoa. Before taking her first bite, she closed her eyes and took a deep breath.

She thought about the farmers who had grown the vegetables, the earth that had nourished them, the sun and rain that had helped them grow. She felt a deep sense of gratitude for the food on her plate, for the effort and care that had gone into bringing it to her table.

As she ate, she focused on each bite, savoring the flavors and textures. She felt a sense of contentment and peace, knowing that she was nourishing her body with wholesome, delicious food.

Over time, Emily's mindful eating practice began to influence other areas of her life. She found herself becoming more mindful in her daily routines, more aware of her actions and choices. She started to slow down, to appreciate the small moments of joy and beauty in everyday life.

She realized that minimalism wasn't just about decluttering her home or simplifying her possessions. It was about living with intention, making conscious choices, and finding joy in the simple things.

One Saturday morning, Emily decided to invite a few friends over for brunch. She wanted to share her newfound love of mindful eating with them, to show them how delicious and satisfying simple, wholesome food could be.

She spent the morning preparing a spread of fresh fruit, whole-grain bread, avocado, and homemade granola. She made a pot of herbal tea and set the table with care, arranging flowers in a vase and placing candles around the room.

When her friends arrived, they were impressed by the beautiful spread. "This looks amazing, Emily!" Sarah exclaimed, reaching for a slice of avocado toast.

"Thanks," Emily replied, smiling. "I've been exploring mindful eating lately, and I wanted to share it with you all."

As they sat down to eat, Emily explained the concept of mindful eating, sharing her experiences and insights. Her friends were intrigued, and they began to discuss their own relationships with food.

"I think I eat too fast," Mark admitted. "I'm always in a hurry, and I don't really take the time to enjoy my food."

"I know what you mean," Sarah added. "I'm always eating on the go, and I don't pay much attention to what I'm eating."

Emily nodded. "I used to be the same way. But since I started practicing mindful eating, I've noticed such a difference. I feel more connected to my food, and I enjoy it so much more."

As they continued to eat and talk, Emily felt a sense of fulfillment and joy. She was grateful for the opportunity to share her journey with her friends, to inspire them to think more mindfully about their own eating habits.

After brunch, as Emily cleaned up the kitchen, she reflected on how far she had come. She had started her minimalist journey feeling overwhelmed and suffocated by her possessions, her digital life, and her hectic schedule. But now, she felt a sense of lightness and freedom, a clarity and peace that she had never experienced before.

She knew that she still had a long way to go, that minimalism was a journey of continuous growth and learning. But she was excited for the road ahead, for the opportunity to continue simplifying her life and living with intention.

As she put away the dishes and wiped down the counter, she felt a deep sense of gratitude—for the food she had eaten, the friends she had shared it with, and the path she was on.

# Chapter 9: A Simplified Routine

Emily's alarm went off at 6:00 a.m., its gentle chime filling the room with a sound that once used to annoy her but now seemed to signal a new beginning. She stretched in her bed, feeling the softness of her sheets and the coolness of the morning air against her skin. Her bedroom was different now—gone were the piles of clothes draped over chairs and the clutter of books and trinkets on her nightstand. The room was sparse, holding only the essentials: a bed, a dresser, and a small plant on the windowsill that caught the morning light.

As she rose to her feet, Emily glanced at her phone, which was now neatly placed on a small wooden shelf by the door. She had started charging it outside her bedroom to avoid the temptation of scrolling through social media late into the night. Her mornings used to start with a rush, her phone guiding her every move with notifications and reminders. Now, they began with silence and a few deep breaths, allowing her to ease into the day.

Walking over to the window, she pulled back the curtain and gazed out at the city. The streets were quiet, the usual morning rush yet to begin. She closed her eyes, savoring the stillness, and began a simple stretching routine she had learned from a YouTube video.

These few moments of movement were something new in her life, an intentional practice she had incorporated into her mornings. Emily found that starting the day with some light stretching helped her feel more awake and connected to her body, shaking off the last vestiges of sleep.

After a few minutes, she headed to the bathroom to wash her face. The bathroom had undergone its own transformation in recent weeks; the once overflowing cabinets were now neatly organized, holding only the essentials. She had donated or discarded the dozens of half-used bottles of shampoo, face creams, and makeup she had accumulated over the years. Now, her skincare routine was simple: a gentle cleanser, a moisturizer, and a swipe of lip balm.

Gone were the days when she would spend over an hour getting ready, carefully applying layers of makeup and styling her hair. Emily now embraced a more natural look, finding that she preferred how she felt without all the fuss. The simplicity of her new routine gave her a sense of freedom and confidence that she hadn't experienced before.

Breakfast Made Simple

Emily made her way to the kitchen, where she had already set out her ingredients for breakfast. She had learned that having a streamlined morning routine involved preparing the night before, setting herself up for a calm and collected start to the day. On the counter sat a small bowl of oats, a banana, and a jar of almond butter—her go-to breakfast for the past few weeks.

She filled a pot with water, set it on the stove, and turned on the heat. While the water boiled, she sliced the banana and laid the pieces neatly in a bowl. Emily found a strange satisfaction in the simplicity of these tasks, a kind of mindfulness she hadn't realized was possible in the mundane act of making breakfast. She watched as the oats began to bubble, the steam rising from the pot, and felt a quiet sense of accomplishment in these small, intentional actions.

Pouring the oats into the bowl, she topped them with banana slices and a spoonful of almond butter. The meal was simple, yet nourishing, providing her with the energy she needed to start her day. She sat down at the small kitchen table and took a moment to appreciate the food in front of her, a habit she had adopted from a book on mindful eating that Aaron had recommended.

As she ate, Emily reflected on how different her mornings had become. Not too long ago, her breakfast routine involved grabbing a hastily prepared coffee and a sugary pastry from the cafe down the street, consuming them on the run as she rushed to work. Now, she took her time, savoring each bite and enjoying the solitude of her morning ritual. It was a small change, but it made a significant impact on her day, setting a tone of calm and intention that she carried with her.

A Wardrobe Revolution

After finishing her breakfast, Emily washed her dishes and placed them in the drying rack, then made her way back to the bedroom to get dressed. Her closet, once a chaotic jumble of clothes, was now a carefully curated collection of pieces she loved and wore regularly. She had adopted a capsule wardrobe, inspired by a minimalist blog she had read early on in her journey. The concept was simple: a small, versatile wardrobe made up of a limited number of pieces that could be mixed and matched in countless ways.

Opening the closet door, Emily scanned her options. Each piece of clothing had earned its place, chosen for its quality, comfort, and versatility. She pulled out a pair of dark jeans and a soft, white blouse, pairing them with a simple necklace and a pair of flats. The outfit was effortless, yet put-together, reflecting her newfound appreciation for simplicity and ease.

Emily glanced at herself in the mirror, smiling at the reflection that looked back. Her mornings were no longer a frantic scramble to find something to wear; instead, they were a deliberate choice, guided by what felt right and comfortable. The capsule wardrobe had not only made getting dressed easier but also helped her redefine her relationship with clothing and consumption.

She had learned that she didn't need an overflowing closet to feel stylish or confident. In fact, having fewer options had made her appreciate her clothes more, each piece serving a purpose and bringing her joy. It was a revelation that had transformed not only her mornings but also her mindset.

Work-Life Balance

Emily grabbed her bag and headed out the door, feeling a sense of calm and readiness as she stepped into the cool morning air. Her commute was a short walk to the subway, a journey she used to dread but now looked forward to.

Instead of mindlessly scrolling through her phone or catching up on work emails, she used the time to listen to podcasts or read, enjoying the opportunity to learn and grow. She had recently started listening to a series on mindfulness and productivity, finding the insights helpful in her quest for a more intentional life.

Arriving at her office building, Emily took a moment to breathe deeply before stepping inside. She had begun incorporating brief moments of mindfulness throughout her day, using them as anchors to keep her grounded amidst the busyness of work.

Her office had also undergone a minimalist makeover; she had cleared her desk of unnecessary papers, trinkets, and gadgets, keeping only what she needed. A laptop, a notebook, and a small plant were all that remained, creating a clean, clutter-free workspace that helped her focus.

Emily sat down and opened her laptop, glancing at her to-do list for the day. She had started using a simple task management app that helped her prioritize her work, breaking her tasks down into manageable chunks. The practice of planning her day with intention had significantly reduced her stress levels, allowing her to approach her work with a sense of clarity and purpose.

She found that by focusing on one task at a time, she was able to accomplish more in less time, freeing up her afternoons for creative projects and personal development. Emily had always been a hard worker, but she now realized that productivity wasn't about doing more; it was about doing less with more focus.

As the day progressed, she maintained her rhythm, taking regular breaks to stretch or walk around the office. She had learned that a simplified routine wasn't just about what she did but also how she did it, incorporating moments of rest and reflection to keep her energy levels up.

Intentional Evenings

At 5:00 p.m., Emily closed her laptop, feeling a sense of satisfaction with her day's work. She had made it a rule to leave the office on time, resisting the urge to stay late and overwork herself. The practice of setting boundaries had been challenging at first, but she found it essential for maintaining a healthy work-life balance.

As she stepped out of the building, she took a moment to appreciate the sunset, its warm hues painting the sky in shades of orange and pink. The beauty of the moment wasn't lost on her; she had learned to find joy in the simple things, savoring the small pleasures that made life meaningful.

On her way home, Emily stopped by the local market to pick up a few groceries for dinner. She had begun cooking more at home, finding it to be a relaxing and rewarding practice. Her meals were simple yet wholesome, made from fresh ingredients that she carefully selected with mindfulness.

Back in her apartment, she unpacked the groceries and set about preparing a stir-fry with vegetables and tofu. The act of cooking was meditative for her, a chance to unwind and focus on the present moment. As she chopped the vegetables and stirred the sizzling tofu, she felt a sense of peace wash over her, the worries of the day melting away.

Dinner was a quiet affair, eaten at her small kitchen table with a view of the city lights. She had made it a habit to eat without distractions, focusing on the flavors and textures of her food. This simple practice of mindful eating had transformed her relationship with food, turning meals into moments of gratitude and appreciation.

After dinner, Emily washed the dishes and tidied up the kitchen, then moved to the living room to relax. She had been reading a book on the philosophy of minimalism, and she enjoyed spending her evenings lost in its pages, finding inspiration and wisdom in its words.

Her nights were no longer filled with the noise of television or the endless scroll of social media. Instead, they were quiet, intentional, and fulfilling, filled with activities that nourished her mind and soul. She had come to realize that a simplified routine wasn't about doing less but about doing what mattered.

The Power of Simplicity

As the evening drew to a close, Emily took a moment to reflect on her day. Her life had changed in so many ways since she began her minimalist journey, each small change adding up to a more intentional, fulfilling existence.

She had discovered the power of simplicity, not just in her physical surroundings but in her daily routines and habits. By eliminating the unnecessary and focusing on what truly mattered, she had created a life that was rich in meaning and purpose.

Emily made her way to the bathroom to brush her teeth, then slipped into bed, feeling the cool sheets against her skin. She reached for her journal on the nightstand, another practice she had incorporated into her evenings. Writing down her thoughts and reflections helped her process the day and set her intentions for tomorrow.

As she wrote, she thought about the impact of her simplified routine, how it had allowed her to reclaim her time and energy, focusing on the things that brought her joy and fulfillment. She had learned that minimalism wasn't about deprivation or sacrifice; it was about making room for what mattered most.

Closing her journal, Emily turned off the light and lay back against the pillows, her mind calm and her heart full. She knew that her journey was far from over, but she felt a deep sense of gratitude for the path she was on. She had found a new way of living, one that embraced simplicity, intention, and joy.

As she drifted off to sleep, she knew that tomorrow would bring its own challenges and opportunities, but she was ready to face them with a clear mind and an open heart. The simplified routine she had created was more than just a series of habits; it was a reflection of her values and a testament to the life she wanted to live.

And for the first time in a long time, Emily felt truly at peace.

# Chapter 10: The Art of Saying No

Emily's apartment was quieter now, reflecting the changes she'd made in her life. The once-crowded shelves were now sparse, holding only a few cherished books and mementos. The space felt liberating, a testament to the progress she had made since starting her minimalist journey.

However, her newfound clarity was about to be tested unexpectedly.

Emily had been invited to three different events over the coming weekend: a friend's birthday party, a networking event for work, and a volunteer meeting for a local environmental group she recently joined. Each event promised to be time-consuming, and the thought of attending all three filled her with dread. Despite her usual enthusiasm, Emily realized she didn't have the energy or the desire to be pulled in so many directions at once.

Sitting on her couch, she glanced at her calendar, the blocks of scheduled activities suddenly looking overwhelming. She knew she couldn't do it all, and more importantly, she didn't want to. The minimalist mantra, "Do less, but better," echoed in her mind. It was a reminder that she could apply minimalism to all aspects of her life, not just her possessions.

But saying no? That was something else entirely.

Emily had always been a people-pleaser, someone who went out of her way to accommodate others, even at her own expense. Growing up, she learned that saying yes was a way to earn approval and avoid disappointment. Declining invitations, even if they were inconvenient or overwhelming, felt like a breach of an unspoken social contract.

But now, with her new approach to life, she recognized the importance of setting boundaries and valuing her time. It was time to learn the art of saying no.

Setting the Stage

The first challenge came when Sarah, a close friend from college, called to remind Emily about her birthday party on Friday night.

"Hey, Em! Just wanted to make sure you're coming to my party this weekend. It's going to be so much fun! I've invited a bunch of people, and it wouldn't be the same without you," Sarah's voice was bright and full of excitement.

Emily hesitated. She loved Sarah and wanted to celebrate her friend's special day, but the thought of a loud, crowded party after a long work week felt draining. She had been looking forward to a quiet Friday night, perhaps reading a book or doing some light yoga. Still, she felt the familiar pull of obligation and guilt creeping in.

"Yeah, of course," Emily replied automatically, her voice lacking the enthusiasm she hoped would mask her reluctance.

"Great! Can't wait to see you!" Sarah chirped before hanging up.

Emily sighed, putting down her phone. She had done it again—committed to something without considering her own needs. As she looked around her simplified living room, she felt a pang of frustration with herself. Why was it so hard to prioritize her own well-being?

Determined to change, she opened her laptop and searched for articles on how to say no gracefully. The advice was straightforward: be honest, keep it simple, and don't over-explain. Emily realized she often felt the need to justify her choices, fearing that a simple "no" would come off as rude or uncaring.

She decided to practice.

Practicing the Art of No

The next opportunity came sooner than expected. During lunch at work the next day, her colleague, Mark, approached her about the networking event.

"Hey, Emily, are you going to that networking thing this weekend? It's supposed to be a big deal, and I think it'd be great for us to make some connections. Plus, free drinks!" Mark grinned, clearly trying to entice her.

Emily took a deep breath, remembering her resolution. She appreciated Mark's enthusiasm, but the event was the last place she wanted to be. She knew that she needed to be honest with him and herself.

"Mark, I've decided not to go. I've been really busy lately, and I'm planning to take it easy this weekend," she said, maintaining eye contact and trying to sound confident.

Mark raised an eyebrow, looking slightly surprised. "Oh? I thought you'd be all over that kind of thing."

Emily smiled gently. "I normally would be, but I've realized I need to recharge this weekend. I'm sure it'll be a great event, though."

To her relief, Mark nodded understandingly. "Yeah, I get it. Sometimes you just need a break. No worries."

Emily felt a rush of relief. Saying no had been uncomfortable, but it also felt liberating. She had made a choice based on what she needed, not on what she thought others expected of her.

Family Expectations

Feeling encouraged, Emily knew she had one more difficult conversation ahead. Her mother had called earlier in the week, inviting her to a family gathering on Sunday. Emily loved her family, but these gatherings were often overwhelming, filled with well-meaning but intrusive questions about her life and career. She wasn't in the mood for a full day of small talk and polite smiling.

Picking up the phone, she called her mother back. As she waited for her to answer, she rehearsed her words, hoping to strike the right balance of honesty and respect.

"Hi, Mom," Emily greeted warmly.

"Hi, sweetheart! I was just thinking about you," her mother replied. "So, are you coming on Sunday? Everyone's excited to see you!"

Emily took another deep breath. "Mom, I'm sorry, but I won't be able to make it this Sunday. I've had a hectic few weeks, and I need some time to rest and recharge."

There was a pause on the other end of the line. Emily could almost hear the wheels turning in her mother's head, trying to figure out how to respond.

"Oh, I see," her mother said slowly. "We were looking forward to seeing you, but I understand. You've been working so hard. Just promise you'll come next time, okay?"

Emily smiled, feeling a mix of relief and gratitude. "Of course, Mom. I'll be there next time. Thanks for understanding."

As she hung up the phone, Emily felt a sense of accomplishment. She had successfully said no to three different commitments without feeling guilty or obligated. It wasn't easy, but it was necessary for her well-being.

Reflecting on the Power of No

That evening, Emily sat in her favorite armchair, a cup of herbal tea in hand. She reflected on the day's events, feeling proud of herself for standing her ground. Saying no had always been difficult for her, but she realized that it was a vital part of her minimalist journey. It was about more than just decluttering her physical space; it was about creating emotional and mental space as well.

By learning to say no, she was taking control of her time and energy, choosing to spend it on things that truly mattered to her. She thought about how often she had said yes out of obligation or fear of disappointing others, only to end up feeling overwhelmed and resentful. But now, she understood that saying no wasn't about rejecting people; it was about honoring her own needs and boundaries.

Emily picked up her journal and began to write:

Today, I learned the art of saying no. It wasn't easy, but it was empowering. I realized that my time and energy are valuable, and I have the right to protect them. Saying no doesn't make me selfish or unkind; it makes me intentional. It allows me to focus on what truly matters and let go of what doesn't. I'm learning to live more authentically, and that starts with being honest about my needs.

As she closed her journal, Emily felt a deep sense of peace. She knew that she still had a lot to learn about setting boundaries and saying no, but she was on the right path. Minimalism was teaching her to live with intention, to choose her actions and commitments mindfully, and to let go of anything that didn't serve her.

An Unexpected Challenge

The next morning, Emily woke up feeling refreshed and energized. She had no plans for the day and decided to take a long walk in the nearby park. As she strolled through the tree-lined paths, she enjoyed the crisp autumn air and the vibrant colors of the falling leaves.

She felt grateful for the time to herself, free from the pressures of her usual obligations. But as she walked, her phone buzzed with a text message. It was from Rachel, a friend she hadn't seen in months.

Rachel: Hey, Emily! I'm in town this weekend and would love to catch up. How about brunch tomorrow?

Emily smiled at the thought of seeing Rachel. They had been close in college but had drifted apart over the years. A part of her was excited at the idea of reconnecting, but another part of her hesitated. She had been looking forward to a quiet weekend and wasn't sure if she wanted to give that up.

She paused, thinking about what she truly wanted. Did she want to spend her Sunday morning at a bustling café, making small talk and catching up? Or did she want to honor her need for rest and solitude?

After a few moments of reflection, Emily decided to be honest with herself and with Rachel. She typed out a reply:

Emily: Hi, Rachel! It's so great to hear from you. I'd love to catch up, but I've been feeling really burnt out lately and need some time to recharge this weekend. How about we plan something for another time? I'd love to see you when I'm feeling more refreshed.

She hit send, feeling a mix of nervousness and relief. It was hard to say no to a friend, especially someone she hadn't seen in a long time. But she knew that she was making the right choice for herself.

A few minutes later, Rachel replied:

Rachel: Totally understand, Emily. No worries at all! Let's catch up soon when you're feeling better. Take care of yourself!

Emily breathed a sigh of relief. She realized that saying no didn't have to be a big deal. Most people were understanding, and those who weren't were likely not worth the stress.

Embracing the Power of No

As Emily continued her walk, she felt a newfound sense of empowerment. She had always feared that saying no would lead to disappointment, rejection, or conflict. But she was beginning to see that it was quite the opposite. Saying no allowed her to be more authentic, to show up fully when she did say yes, and to build stronger, more honest relationships.

She thought about all the times she had overcommitted herself, stretching herself thin to please others or meet expectations. Those moments often left her feeling exhausted, resentful, and disconnected from her own needs. But now, she was learning to prioritize herself without guilt or shame.

Emily realized that saying no was an act of self-care, a way to protect her energy and focus on what truly mattered. It was about choosing quality over quantity, depth over breadth, and meaning over obligation.

She decided that from now on, she would be more intentional with her commitments, only saying yes to things that aligned with her values and brought her joy. She would no longer feel pressured to do things out of guilt, obligation, or fear of missing out.

Emily smiled as she reached the end of the park trail, feeling lighter and more at peace than she had in a long time. She knew that she was still a work in progress, but she was proud of the steps she was taking to live more authentically.

A New Beginning

Over the next few weeks, Emily continued to practice the art of saying no. She declined unnecessary meetings at work, opted out of social events that didn't interest her, and set boundaries with friends and family. Each time she said no, she felt a little more confident and a little more in control of her life.

She noticed that by saying no more often, she had more time and energy to devote to the things that truly mattered to her. She spent more time on her hobbies, deepened her relationships with a select few friends, and focused on her personal growth.

Emily's life wasn't perfect, but it was becoming more aligned with her values and desires. She was learning to live with intention, to make choices based on what she needed rather than what others expected of her.

One evening, as she sat down to meditate, Emily reflected on her journey. She thought about how far she had come since she first discovered minimalism and how much she had learned about herself in the process. She realized that minimalism wasn't just about decluttering her physical space; it was about decluttering her mind, her time, and her life.

By letting go of what didn't serve her, she was creating space for what did. She was learning to say no to the things that didn't matter, so she could say yes to the things that did.

As she closed her eyes and focused on her breath, Emily felt a deep sense of peace and gratitude. She knew that the art of saying no was a lifelong practice, one that required mindfulness, courage, and self-compassion. But she was ready for the challenge.

After all, she had already taken the first step: she had said yes to herself.

# Chapter 11: Minimalist Travels

Emily zipped up her backpack, marveling at how light it felt on her shoulders. Just a few months ago, the idea of traveling with only one bag would have been unthinkable. Her usual routine involved multiple suitcases filled to the brim with outfit choices, shoes for every possible occasion, and just-in-case items she rarely if ever, used. Now, as she looked down at her minimalist packing list, she felt a thrill of excitement at the prospect of traveling with so little.

Aaron had encouraged her to take a minimalist trip. "It's the ultimate test," he had said over coffee a few weeks earlier. "It challenges you to prioritize your needs over your wants and forces you to focus on experiences rather than possessions."

Emily was skeptical at first. How could she possibly enjoy a trip without all the comforts she was used to? But the more she thought about it, the more she realized that her previous travels had often been overshadowed by stress and frustration – lost luggage, long waits at baggage claim, and the constant worry of forgetting something. Maybe there was something to this minimalist travel idea.

So here she was, standing in her living room with only a small backpack, ready to embark on a week-long trip to Lisbon, Portugal. Her packing list was simple: a few versatile outfits, comfortable shoes, a small toiletry kit, her journal, and a Kindle loaded with books. She felt a sense of freedom she hadn't anticipated, a lightness that extended beyond the weight of her bag.

As she made her way to the airport, Emily couldn't help but notice how different this experience was from her usual pre-travel frenzy.

Instead of rushing around, she had time to enjoy a leisurely breakfast and a cup of coffee at her favorite café. There was no frantic last-minute packing, no worrying about whether her suitcase would be overweight. Everything she needed was already with her.

At the airport, she breezed through security, skipping the long lines at check-in. For the first time, she understood what Aaron meant when he said that minimalist travel allowed you to focus on the journey, not just the destination.

The flight to Lisbon was uneventful, and Emily spent most of the time reading a novel she had downloaded onto her Kindle. She found herself smiling at the simplicity of it all – just her, a book, and the anticipation of exploring a new city.

When she arrived in Lisbon, the sun was just beginning to set, casting a golden glow over the city's red rooftops and cobblestone streets. Emily took a deep breath, savoring the warm, salty air. She felt a sense of calm wash over her, a feeling she hadn't experienced on previous trips. Maybe it was the lack of baggage, or perhaps it was her newfound focus on being present, but whatever it was, she was grateful for it.

Emily's accommodation was a small, charming guesthouse tucked away in the heart of the Alfama district. She had chosen it for its simplicity – a cozy room with a bed, a desk, and a window that opened onto a narrow street lined with colorful buildings. As she set down her backpack, she felt a wave of contentment. There was no need to unpack or organize. She had everything she needed, and that was enough.

The next morning, Emily set out to explore the city with nothing but her small crossbody bag and a water bottle. She wandered through the winding streets of Alfama, marveling at the tile-covered facades and the vibrant street art that seemed to adorn every corner. Without the burden of a heavy bag, she moved freely, weaving in and out of shops and cafes, stopping whenever something caught her eye.

She quickly realized that minimalist travel was more than just packing light; it was a mindset. Instead of rushing from one tourist attraction to another, she allowed herself to be guided by curiosity and intuition. She spent hours sitting in a small café, sipping espresso and watching the world go by. She struck up a conversation with a local artist who was sketching in the plaza, learning about the city's rich history and culture.

As the days went by, Emily found herself shedding not just physical possessions, but also the need for constant activity. She embraced the art of doing nothing, of simply being present in the moment. One afternoon, she took a tram up to the Miradouro de Santa Catarina, a lookout point with a stunning view of the city and the Tagus River. She spent hours there, basking in the warm sun, watching the boats drift by, and listening to the distant sounds of Fado music echoing through the streets.

For the first time in her life, Emily felt truly free. Free from the weight of possessions, from the pressure to do and see everything, from the need to capture every moment on camera. She realized that the most meaningful experiences were often the simplest ones – a quiet morning walk along the river, a shared smile with a stranger, the taste of a freshly baked pastel de nata.

One evening, as Emily was enjoying a glass of wine at a small tapas bar, she met a fellow traveler named Leo. He was a photographer from Argentina, traveling through Europe with nothing but a small camera bag and a few changes of clothes. They struck up a conversation, and Emily was fascinated by his stories of minimalist travel. Leo explained that for him, minimalism was about more than just material possessions; it was about capturing the essence of a place, of distilling a city's soul into a single image.

"Traveling light allows me to move freely," he said, gesturing to his compact camera. "I'm not weighed down by equipment or expectations. I can go where the light takes me, follow my instincts, and connect with the people I meet."

Emily nodded, understanding exactly what he meant. In the past, her travels had been about ticking off boxes, capturing perfect photos, and sharing them on social media. But now, she realized that the true joy of travel came from being fully present, from experiencing a place with all her senses, without the need for validation or approval.

As the night wore on, Emily and Leo shared stories of their journeys, their dreams, and their newfound appreciation for simplicity. It was refreshing to connect with someone who shared her values, who understood the freedom that came from letting go.

The next morning, Emily woke up early and decided to take a day trip to Sintra, a small town known for its fairytale-like palaces and gardens. She packed a light snack, her water bottle, and her journal, and set off on the train. As she made her way through the lush hills and misty forests, she felt a deep sense of peace. There was no rush, no itinerary, just the simple pleasure of exploring a new place.

Sintra was everything she had hoped for and more. She spent the day wandering through the enchanting gardens of Quinta da Regaleira, climbing the winding staircases of the Palácio da Pena, and soaking in the breathtaking views from the Moorish Castle. With her minimalist mindset, she found herself appreciating the details she might have overlooked in the past – the intricate tilework, the scent of blooming flowers, the sound of birds singing in the trees.

As the sun began to set, Emily made her way back to the train station, feeling a profound sense of gratitude. This trip had been a revelation, a reminder that the most meaningful experiences often came from the simplest of moments. She realized that minimalism wasn't about depriving herself of experiences, but rather about enriching them by focusing on what truly mattered.

Back in Lisbon, Emily spent her final days savoring the city's delights. She indulged in fresh seafood at a local market, danced to live Fado music in a dimly lit tavern, and watched the sunset from the iconic Belém Tower. With each passing day, she felt more connected to the city, more attuned to its rhythm and spirit.

On her last evening, Emily found herself back at the Miradouro de Santa Catarina, watching the city lights twinkle against the darkening sky. She thought about all the things she had learned on this trip – the importance of presence, the joy of simplicity, the freedom of letting go. She realized that minimalist travel wasn't just a way to see the world; it was a way to live.

As she gazed out at the city below, Emily felt a deep sense of fulfillment. She knew that this journey was just the beginning, that there were countless more adventures to be had, more lessons to be learned. But for now, she was content to simply be, to savor the moment and embrace the beauty of the present.

The next morning, Emily packed her backpack and headed to the airport, feeling a mix of nostalgia and excitement. She knew that returning home didn't mean returning to her old ways. This trip had changed her, had opened her eyes to the possibilities of a life lived with intention and purpose.

As the plane took off, Emily looked out the window, watching Lisbon fade into the distance. She felt a sense of peace wash over her, knowing that she was carrying with her the lessons of this journey, the memories of a city that had taught her the value of less.

For the first time, she truly understood the meaning of minimalism. It wasn't about giving up, but about gaining so much more – more freedom, more clarity, more joy.

# Chapter 12: Living with Intention

Emily sat cross-legged on the floor of her minimalist apartment, the morning sun casting a golden hue over the walls. A gentle breeze wafted in from the open window, bringing with it the scent of fresh grass and flowers from the park below. The apartment was serene and uncluttered, with only a few pieces of furniture and a handful of carefully chosen decorations. A sense of calmness enveloped Emily, a stark contrast to the chaos that had once dominated her life.

After months of decluttering, simplifying, and learning to let go, Emily had reached a new phase in her minimalist journey. She no longer felt the compulsive urge to fill every corner of her life with things, nor did she feel weighed down by the expectations of consumer culture. But as she looked around her pared-down space, she realized there was still a lingering question: What now?

Aaron, her mentor and friend, had posed a challenge to her recently. "Minimalism is more than just getting rid of stuff," he had said over coffee. "It's about creating space for what truly matters. Have you thought about what you want to fill your life with now that you've made so much room?"

The question had caught Emily off guard. In her excitement over her newfound simplicity, she hadn't really considered the deeper aspects of what minimalism could mean. She had focused so much on letting go that she hadn't yet thought about what she wanted to hold onto.

"Living with intention," Aaron had continued, "means making choices based on your values and what brings you joy, rather than what you think you should do or have. It's about aligning your actions with your true self."

That conversation had stuck with Emily, and now, sitting in the quiet of her apartment, she decided it was time to take a closer look at her life. She reached for her journal, a plain, leather-bound notebook she had chosen deliberately for its simplicity and quality. Flipping to a fresh page, she wrote at the top:

What do I truly value?

She stared at the page, the pen hovering in her hand. The answer wasn't as obvious as she'd expected. For years, her values had been shaped by external influences: career success, material wealth, and the approval of others. But as she had stripped away the clutter from her life, she realized that many of these values no longer resonated with her.

After a moment's hesitation, she began to write:

Connection: Building meaningful relationships with people who bring out the best in me.Growth: Continuously learning and evolving, both personally and professionally.Health: Nurturing my body and mind through mindful practices and self-care.Contribution: Making a positive impact on my community and the world.

As she wrote, Emily felt a sense of clarity forming within her. These values were the core of who she wanted to be and how she wanted to live. But living with intention meant more than just identifying values; it required her to act on them, to make choices that reflected these priorities.

With a renewed sense of purpose, Emily decided to take a day to reflect deeply on how she could incorporate these values into her daily life. She wanted to ensure that every decision, big or small, aligned with the person she was becoming.

The next morning, Emily awoke with a plan. She brewed a cup of herbal tea, enjoying the simplicity of the ritual, and set out to explore the city with fresh eyes. She wasn't looking for distractions or purchases; instead, she wanted to observe and experience the world with intention.

She made her way to the community garden a few blocks away, a place she had passed countless times but never truly noticed. As she entered the garden, she was greeted by a symphony of colors—vibrant reds, yellows, and purples of blooming flowers, the rich green of leafy vegetables, and the earthy browns of freshly tilled soil.

A group of volunteers was busy weeding and watering, their hands moving deftly as they chatted and laughed. Emily approached them, feeling a sudden urge to connect. "Hi, I'm Emily," she said, smiling. "I've walked by here so many times but never came in. It's beautiful."

An older woman with silver hair and bright blue eyes looked up from her work. "Welcome, Emily! I'm Susan. We're always happy to have new faces here. Would you like to help out?"

Emily nodded, feeling a spark of excitement. "I'd love to."

Susan handed her a pair of gloves and showed her how to tend to the plants. As Emily worked, she felt a sense of fulfillment that she hadn't experienced in a long time. There was something grounding about being in the garden, connecting with the earth and with people who shared her desire to contribute to something greater.

As the morning passed, Emily got to know the other volunteers, learning about their lives and why they chose to spend their time in the garden. Some were there to escape the hustle of city life, others to learn about sustainable living, and a few simply enjoyed the companionship.

Emily found herself deeply moved by their stories and realized that this was what she had been missing—a sense of community, of belonging to something meaningful. By the time she left the garden, her hands were dirty, her clothes were smudged, but her heart felt full.

Walking home, Emily reflected on the experience. She had spent just a few hours in the garden, but the impact was profound. She had connected with new people, learned new skills, and contributed to her community, all of which aligned perfectly with her values. It was a powerful reminder of how living with intention could transform even the simplest of activities into something meaningful.

Over the next few weeks, Emily continued to explore what living with intention meant for her. She started by revisiting her daily routines, identifying areas where she could make more mindful choices. She realized that many of her habits were driven by convenience or habit rather than purpose.

One area she decided to focus on was her mornings. She had fallen into the habit of waking up and immediately checking her phone, scrolling through social media and emails before she even got out of bed. It was a mindless routine that often left her feeling frazzled before the day had even begun.

Determined to create a more intentional start to her day, Emily decided to implement a morning routine that aligned with her values of health and growth. She began waking up a little earlier, allowing herself time to meditate and set an intention for the day. She practiced yoga, savoring the stretch and flow of her body as she moved through the poses. Afterward, she made herself a nutritious breakfast, enjoying each bite without the distraction of screens.

This new routine transformed her mornings. Instead of starting her day with stress and overwhelm, she began each day feeling grounded, focused, and energized. She noticed that her productivity at work improved, and she was more present in her interactions with colleagues and friends.

Emily also took a closer look at her professional life. She had always been driven by the desire to climb the corporate ladder, to achieve more, earn more, and be seen as successful. But as she reflected on her values, she realized that this drive was no longer aligned with who she wanted to be.

She began to question the long hours and the constant push for more, wondering if there was a way to find fulfillment without sacrificing her well-being. Inspired by her new perspective, Emily approached her manager with a proposal to work more flexible hours, allowing her to pursue her passions outside of work while still contributing effectively to her team.

To her surprise, her manager was supportive. "We've noticed how focused and productive you've been lately," he said. "If this arrangement helps you maintain that balance, I'm all for it."

With her new schedule in place, Emily found herself with more time to explore her interests and deepen her connections with others. She started attending local workshops on sustainable living and joined a book club focused on personal growth and mindfulness. These activities not only aligned with her values but also brought her immense joy and satisfaction.

As Emily continued to make intentional choices, she found herself becoming more attuned to the world around her. She noticed the beauty in everyday moments—the way the sunlight filtered through the trees, the sound of birds singing in the morning, the laughter of children playing in the park. These simple pleasures, which she had often overlooked in the past, now filled her with a deep sense of gratitude.

One evening, as she sat on her balcony watching the sunset, Emily reflected on how much her life had changed since she first discovered minimalism. She had started with the goal of decluttering her space, but in the process, she had decluttered her mind and heart as well. By letting go of the unnecessary, she had made room for what truly mattered: connection, growth, health, and contribution.

The concept of living with intention became a guiding principle for Emily, influencing every aspect of her life. It wasn't always easy—there were moments when she felt tempted to revert to old habits or when she struggled to maintain her focus on what truly mattered. But each time, she reminded herself of her values and the joy she found in aligning her actions with them.

One day, Aaron invited Emily to join him on a hike in the nearby mountains. As they ascended the trail, surrounded by towering trees and the sounds of nature, Aaron turned to her and said, "You've come a long way, Emily. How does it feel?"

Emily smiled, taking in the crisp, fresh air. "It feels liberating. I've realized that living with intention isn't about being perfect or having everything figured out. It's about making choices that reflect who I am and what I believe in. It's about being present and mindful in each moment."

Aaron nodded. "That's exactly it. Minimalism isn't a destination; it's a journey. And as you've discovered, it's a journey that leads to a deeper understanding of yourself and the world around you."

As they reached the summit, Emily gazed out at the breathtaking view before them—the vast expanse of forest, the rolling hills, and the distant glimmer of the ocean. She felt a profound sense of peace, knowing that she was exactly where she was meant to be.

In that moment, Emily realized that living with intention wasn't just about making choices aligned with her values; it was about embracing the fullness of life, with all its beauty and complexity. It was about finding joy in the present moment, appreciating the journey, and trusting that by living authentically, she was creating a life of purpose and fulfillment.

# Chapter 13: Resistance from the Past

Emily had been preparing for her parents' visit for weeks. The upcoming weekend would mark the first time they would see her new, minimalist apartment, and Emily was anxious. She loved her parents deeply, but she knew their views were firmly rooted in traditional values — ones that emphasized stability, comfort, and material success. Growing up, her parents had always associated a well-furnished home with prosperity and a sign that one had "made it." Emily had benefited from this mindset, living in a spacious house with plenty of toys, gadgets, and clothing. Her parents had worked hard for every bit of luxury they afforded, and they took pride in providing their daughter with everything she could ever need.

However, her new apartment was different. Emily had deliberately chosen a smaller, simpler space that she could easily manage. Her belongings were pared down to the essentials, each item carefully selected for its function and meaning. It was a stark contrast to the home she grew up in, and she was unsure how her parents would react.

As she finished dusting the last shelf, Emily's phone buzzed on the kitchen counter. It was her mother, confirming their arrival time. They would be there in an hour.

Emily glanced around her apartment one last time, taking in the minimalist décor. The living room held a single, comfortable couch, a small coffee table, and a plant by the window. Her kitchen was similarly sparse, with only the most essential appliances visible. Even her bedroom, the most personal space, was modest — just a bed, a lamp, and a narrow bookshelf filled with her favorite reads.

She took a deep breath, trying to calm the flutter of nerves in her stomach. "It's just an apartment," she told herself. "It's a reflection of who I am now, not who I used to be."

But deep down, she knew it was more than that. This visit was a test of sorts, a confrontation between her old life and her new one. And no matter how much she tried to prepare herself, she couldn't shake the feeling that she was about to step into a storm.

The doorbell rang, and Emily's heart leaped into her throat. She smoothed her hair nervously and opened the door.

"Emily!" her mother exclaimed, pulling her into a tight hug. Her father, standing just behind, smiled warmly and gave her a pat on the back.

"Hi, Mom. Hi, Dad," Emily said, returning their embrace. "Come on in."

As they stepped inside, Emily watched their faces closely. Her mother's eyes swept across the room, lingering on the bare walls and the lack of knick-knacks. Her father's brow furrowed slightly as he noticed the absence of a television.

"What a... cozy place you have," her mother finally said, trying to sound cheerful.

"Thanks," Emily replied, forcing a smile. "I like to keep things simple."

Her father gave a small nod but didn't say anything. Emily could sense his discomfort as he looked around the apartment, his gaze landing on the empty spaces where furniture or decorations might traditionally be.

"So, what do you think?" Emily asked, her voice tinged with nervousness. She wanted them to understand, to see the beauty and peace she had found in her minimalist lifestyle.

Her mother hesitated before answering. "Well, it's certainly... different from what we're used to," she said carefully. "It's very... minimal."

Emily nodded, acknowledging the truth in her mother's words. "I've found that I don't need much to be happy," she explained. "Living with less has helped me focus on what's important."

Her father finally spoke up, his voice low and cautious. "Are you sure you're okay, Emily? I mean, is everything going alright at work? Do you need any help?"

Emily's heart sank at his words. She knew they meant well, but their concern felt like a lack of faith in her choices. "I'm fine, Dad. Really. I'm doing great at work, and I love my job. This is just... the way I've chosen to live now."

Her father exchanged a worried glance with her mother. "It just seems so... sparse," he said. "Like you're missing out on things."

Emily took a deep breath, trying to remain calm. She had anticipated this reaction, but it still stung. "I'm not missing out on anything, Dad. I've gained so much more by letting go of what I don't need. I have more time, more freedom, more peace of mind."

Her mother's face softened slightly, but her eyes were still filled with concern. "But what about comfort, honey? Don't you want to have a few nice things? You used to love decorating your room with all those little trinkets and photos."

Emily smiled gently. "I did, Mom. And those things were important to me back then. But I've realized that I don't need a lot of stuff to feel comfortable or happy. I'd rather have a few things that truly matter to me than a lot of things that don't."

Her father sighed, shaking his head. "I just don't understand, Emily. We worked so hard to give you everything you could ever want. And now it feels like you're... rejecting all of that."

Emily's chest tightened at his words. She knew this was the heart of their discomfort — the feeling that her choice to live minimally was a rejection of their efforts and their love.

"I'm not rejecting anything, Dad," she said softly. "I'm so grateful for everything you and Mom have given me. You taught me the value of hard work and the importance of providing for yourself. But I've also learned that happiness doesn't come from things. It comes from within."

Her mother reached out and took her hand. "We just want you to be happy, sweetheart. And if this is what makes you happy, then we'll try to understand."

Emily squeezed her mother's hand, feeling a swell of gratitude. "Thank you, Mom. That means a lot to me."

Her father still looked troubled, but he nodded slowly. "I guess we all have to find our own way in life," he said. "Just promise us you'll let us know if you need anything. We're always here for you."

"I promise," Emily said, her voice steady. "And I'm always here for you, too."

After her parents settled in, Emily took them on a tour of the apartment, pointing out the few items that held special significance for her. Her parents listened attentively, trying to understand her perspective, even if they didn't fully grasp it.

In the kitchen, Emily brewed a pot of tea, and they sat down together at the small dining table. The atmosphere was more relaxed now, the initial shock of her lifestyle choice beginning to fade.

"So, tell us more about this minimalist thing," her father said, his tone more curious than concerned now. "How did you get into it?"

Emily smiled, relieved that they were opening up to the idea. "It all started when I realized how overwhelmed I was by my stuff. My apartment was so cluttered, and it made me feel stressed all the time. I stumbled across a blog about minimalism, and it just clicked for me. I decided to give it a try, and I've never looked back."

Her mother nodded slowly. "I can see how having less clutter might help you feel calmer. I've been meaning to declutter the attic for years, but I just can't seem to let go of things."

"That's exactly it," Emily said, leaning forward. "It's not just about getting rid of stuff. It's about letting go of the things that don't add value to your life, so you can focus on what matters."

Her father stroked his chin thoughtfully. "I suppose that makes sense. But what about when you want to entertain guests? Don't you feel like you need more... I don't know, more stuff?"

Emily chuckled. "You'd be surprised how much fun you can have with just a few friends, a simple meal, and some good conversation. I've found that it's not the things you have that make a gathering special; it's the people and the memories you create together."

Her mother's eyes softened, and she reached out to squeeze Emily's hand again. "You've always been wise beyond your years, Emily. I guess your father and I just need to catch up."

Emily felt a surge of emotion at her mother's words. She knew this was a big step for them, and she appreciated their willingness to try to understand.

"I'm really glad you're both here," she said, her voice thick with emotion. "It means a lot to me."

"We wouldn't miss it for the world," her father said, giving her a reassuring smile.

As the evening wore on, the conversation turned to lighter topics, and Emily felt a sense of relief. Her parents were trying, and that was all she could ask for. They might not fully understand her choices yet, but they were willing to support her, and that meant everything.

Later, as Emily showed them to the guest room, her mother paused in the doorway. "You know, Emily," she said softly, "I think there's something we can learn from you. Maybe it's time for your father and me to start letting go of some things, too."

Emily smiled, her heart swelling with love for her mother. "You don't have to change anything you're not ready for, Mom. Minimalism isn't about getting rid of everything. It's about finding what works for you."

Her mother nodded, a thoughtful look in her eyes. "Still, I think there's something to be said for living with less. Maybe it's time we tried it out."

Emily hugged her mother tightly, feeling a sense of peace she hadn't felt in a long time. "Whatever you decide, I'll be here to support you," she said.

As she watched her parents settle into the guest room, Emily felt a weight lift off her shoulders. It hadn't been easy, but she had faced the resistance from her past and come out stronger on the other side. Her parents might not fully understand her choices yet, but they were willing to try, and that was more than enough.

She closed the door quietly and made her way back to the living room, feeling a renewed sense of calm. The storm had passed, and in its wake, Emily felt a deeper connection to her parents and to herself. She knew the journey ahead wouldn't always be easy, but she was ready to face it, one step at a time.

With a contented sigh, Emily settled onto the couch, pulling a blanket around her shoulders. The city outside her window was quiet, the streetlights casting a soft glow on the empty streets. For the first time in a long time, Emily felt truly at home — not just in her apartment, but in her skin.

As she drifted off to sleep, Emily couldn't help but smile. She was living a life that felt true to her, a life that was simple, intentional, and full of meaning. And that, she realized, was all she needed.

The next morning, Emily woke up early, feeling refreshed and eager to spend more time with her parents. She found them already in the kitchen, her mother making breakfast while her father read the newspaper.

"Good morning!" Emily said cheerfully as she joined them.

"Good morning, honey," her mother replied, smiling. "I hope you don't mind — I thought I'd whip up some pancakes."

"Not at all," Emily said, feeling a warm glow at the sight of her mother bustling around her kitchen. "It smells wonderful."

As they sat down to eat, Emily noticed her father watching her with a thoughtful expression. "What is it, Dad?" she asked, tilting her head.

He hesitated for a moment before speaking. "I was just thinking about what you said yesterday, about finding happiness within and not through things. I've always believed in working hard and providing for my family, but I guess I never thought about what comes after that. Maybe it's time I did."

Emily reached across the table to take his hand. "It's never too late to start, Dad. And it doesn't have to be all or nothing. You can take small steps and see what feels right for you."

Her father nodded slowly, a small smile tugging at his lips. "Maybe I'll start by cleaning out the garage. Your mother's been after me to do that for years."

Emily laughed, feeling a surge of affection for her parents. They might not fully understand her minimalist lifestyle, but they were trying, and that was more than enough.

As they finished breakfast and cleared the table, Emily felt a sense of contentment she hadn't felt in a long time. She had faced resistance from her past, and while there was still work to be done, she knew she was on the right path.

Later, as they prepared to leave, her mother pulled her into a tight hug. "We're so proud of you, Emily," she whispered. "You're living your truth, and that's all we've ever wanted for you."

Tears welled up in Emily's eyes as she hugged her mother back. "Thank you, Mom. That means the world to me."

# Chapter 14: The Decline of Convenience

Emily sat at her minimalist desk in her small, uncluttered apartment, typing away on her laptop. The morning sun streamed through the window, casting a soft glow on the freshly painted white walls. Her once chaotic space now felt like a sanctuary, a place where she could think clearly and live intentionally. But today, despite the calm environment, Emily felt restless. She was grappling with a realization that had been nagging at her for days: minimalism wasn't always convenient.

Since embracing a minimalist lifestyle, Emily had learned to let go of many things she once thought were essential. She no longer felt the need to buy the latest gadgets or follow every trend. Her life was simpler, and she was happier for it. Yet, as she discovered, living with less often meant doing things the hard way.

This realization struck her most acutely when she tried to cook a meal from scratch the night before. She had decided to make a simple vegetable stir-fry with ingredients she bought from the local farmers' market. It seemed like an easy enough task, but as she rummaged through her minimal kitchen, she realized she lacked the right tools. Her old wok had been donated months ago, and she hadn't bothered to replace it, believing that fewer kitchen gadgets would streamline her cooking. She ended up using a small pan, which took twice as long and resulted in unevenly cooked vegetables.

As she sat there chewing on slightly burnt broccoli, she couldn't help but think back to her old life when she would have easily ordered takeout. Convenience had once been her best friend—one-click shopping, food delivery apps, and same-day shipping. Everything she could possibly want was at her fingertips. Now, she was beginning to see the cracks in her minimalist lifestyle.

Emily's phone buzzed, pulling her from her thoughts. It was a text from her friend Lily. "Hey! Wanna grab coffee later today?"

Lily was one of the few friends who supported Emily's minimalist journey. While many had questioned her choices or teased her about her 'extreme' lifestyle changes, Lily had always been encouraging. But even she didn't fully understand the trade-offs Emily had been making.

Emily replied, "Sure, I'd love to. How about that little café on Elm Street?"

"Sounds great! See you at 3!"

Putting her phone down, Emily turned back to her work. She had recently started freelancing as a writer, having left her high-stress corporate job a few months ago. The decision to leave had been another step toward a minimalist life. She wanted to spend her days doing something she loved, something that aligned with her new values.

However, freelancing came with its own set of challenges. She no longer had a steady paycheck, which meant budgeting was tighter than ever. She had to be meticulous with her spending, scrutinizing every expense to ensure it aligned with her needs and values. The days of convenient, impulse buys were over.

The clock ticked closer to 3 PM, and Emily wrapped up her work. She grabbed her tote bag, slipped on her shoes, and headed out the door. The café was only a ten-minute walk away, another conscious choice she had made to cut down on unnecessary car trips and embrace a more eco-friendly lifestyle. As she walked, she felt the crisp autumn air brush against her face. It was a refreshing change from the stale, air-conditioned environment of her former office.

When she arrived at the café, Lily was already there, seated at a small table by the window. She waved and smiled as Emily approached.

"Hey! How's it going?" Lily asked.

"Good, good. Just trying to balance work and life, you know," Emily replied as she sat down.

They chatted for a while, catching up on the latest happenings in their lives. Emily sipped her coffee, savoring the rich flavor. It was a rare treat, something she allowed herself every now and then. She had learned to appreciate the small pleasures in life, finding joy in simple moments like this.

"So, how's the minimalist life treating you?" Lily asked.

Emily hesitated for a moment, considering her response. "It's... different," she said finally. "I mean, I love the freedom it's given me. I feel less tied down by things and more focused on what really matters. But... it's not always easy."

Lily raised an eyebrow. "What do you mean?"

"Well, take last night for example," Emily said. "I tried to cook dinner, but I realized I didn't have the right pan. I ended up using this tiny one that took forever, and the food didn't come out great. If I still had all my old kitchen stuff, it would have been so much easier."

Lily nodded sympathetically. "Yeah, I guess that's one downside. You're giving up some convenience for simplicity."

"Exactly," Emily agreed. "And it's not just cooking. It's everything. Sometimes I miss the ease of just ordering something online without a second thought or driving somewhere instead of walking. I know it's all for a good reason, but it's hard to let go of those comforts."

They sat in silence for a moment, both lost in thought. Finally, Lily spoke up. "You know, I think it's about finding a balance. Minimalism doesn't have to mean depriving yourself of everything convenient. Maybe it's more about being intentional with what you choose to keep and what you let go."

Emily nodded, considering Lily's words. She had always seen minimalism as an all-or-nothing approach, but maybe there was room for flexibility. She didn't have to sacrifice every convenience to live a meaningful life. It was about making conscious choices that aligned with her values, not following a rigid set of rules.

As they finished their coffee, Emily felt a sense of clarity. She didn't have to be perfect in her minimalist journey. She could allow herself some conveniences, as long as they didn't detract from her overall goals. It was about finding a balance that worked for her.

They said their goodbyes, and Emily headed back home, feeling lighter than she had in days. She still believed in the power of minimalism, but she was ready to approach it with a more open mind.

When she got home, she decided to tackle a task she had been putting off for weeks: organizing her kitchen. She opened the cabinets and pulled out everything inside, laying it all out on the counter. As she went through each item, she asked herself if it truly served a purpose in her life.

She kept the essentials—a few pots and pans, some basic utensils, and a handful of dishes. But she also allowed herself to keep a couple of 'non-essential' items, like a small blender she used occasionally and a waffle maker that brought her joy on lazy Sunday mornings.

It wasn't about having the bare minimum. It was about having what she needed and nothing more.

After an hour of sorting and organizing, Emily stepped back to admire her work. Her kitchen looked clean and orderly, but not sparse. It was a space that reflected her values and her personality—a balance between simplicity and practicality.

Feeling accomplished, she decided to reward herself with a relaxing evening. She brewed a cup of herbal tea and settled onto her couch with a book she had borrowed from the library. As she sipped her tea and turned the pages, she felt a sense of peace wash over her. She was living a life that was true to her, a life that brought her joy and fulfillment.

The next morning, Emily woke up with a renewed sense of purpose. She had come to terms with the challenges of minimalism and was ready to embrace them. She knew that living with less wasn't always convenient, but it was worth it. It allowed her to focus on what truly mattered, to live with intention and clarity.

She spent the day working on her freelance projects, feeling more focused and productive than ever. In the afternoon, she took a break to prepare a simple lunch—this time with the right pan. As she cooked, she thought about the conversation with Lily and the insights it had brought.

Minimalism wasn't about deprivation or sacrifice. It was about living in a way that aligned with her values, making intentional choices that brought her closer to the life she wanted. It was okay to keep some conveniences, as long as they didn't become a crutch or a distraction.

As she sat down to eat, Emily felt a deep sense of gratitude. She was grateful for the journey she had embarked on, for the lessons she had learned, and for the person she was becoming. She knew there would be more challenges ahead, but she was ready to face them with an open heart and a clear mind.

The days passed, and Emily continued to refine her minimalist lifestyle. She learned to navigate the balance between convenience and simplicity, finding what worked best for her. She kept the conveniences that added value to her life and let go of those that didn't.

She also began to share her experiences more openly with others. She started a blog to document her journey, writing about the ups and downs of minimalism and the lessons she had learned. She was surprised by how many people resonated with her story, reaching out to share their own experiences and struggles.

Through her blog, Emily found a sense of community and support. She realized she wasn't alone in her quest for a simpler, more meaningful life. There were others who shared her values and were also seeking a path away from consumerism and excess.

One day, she received an email from a reader named Sam. He wrote about how he had been inspired by her blog to start decluttering his own life. He had always felt overwhelmed by his possessions and the constant pressure to buy more, but reading Emily's story gave him the courage to make a change.

As Emily read Sam's email, she felt a surge of joy. She had always hoped her journey would inspire others, but she hadn't expected it to happen so soon. She replied to Sam, thanking him for his kind words and encouraging him to keep going.

That night, as Emily lay in bed, she thought about the impact she was having. She realized that minimalism wasn't just about her own life; it was about creating a ripple effect, inspiring others to live with intention and purpose.

She felt a deep sense of fulfillment, knowing she was making a difference. She drifted off to sleep, dreaming of a world where people valued experiences over possessions, where they lived with less but felt more.

The next morning, Emily woke up feeling refreshed and energized. She was ready to continue her journey, embracing the challenges and joys of minimalism. She knew it wouldn't always be easy, but she was committed to living a life that aligned with her values.

As she got ready for the day, she smiled to herself, thinking about how far she had come. She had learned to let go of convenience and embrace simplicity, to find joy in the little things and live with intention.

She was living a life that was true to her, a life that brought her peace and fulfillment. And for that, she was grateful.

Emily sat down at her desk, ready to tackle the day's work. She opened her laptop and began typing, feeling a sense of purpose and clarity. She knew she was on the right path, and she was excited to see where it would lead.

She was living the minimalist life, and she wouldn't have it any other way.

# Chapter 15: Overcoming Burnout

Emily sat in her living room, staring blankly at her laptop screen. The cursor blinked impatiently on an empty page, a stark contrast to the storm of thoughts raging in her mind. Her to-do list had grown exponentially over the past few weeks, and despite her best efforts to prioritize and simplify, she found herself overwhelmed.

She had committed to too much, yet again. Meetings at work, organizing minimalist meet-ups, volunteering at the local shelter, and trying to keep up with her decluttering journey—all had become too much to handle. The simplicity she had once craved now felt like a distant memory, replaced by a growing sense of fatigue and frustration.

"I'm supposed to feel lighter," Emily muttered to herself. "Not like I'm drowning in commitments."

The irony was not lost on her. In her quest to live a minimalist life, she had inadvertently overburdened herself with tasks and responsibilities, each one more important than the last. The idea of "doing less with more focus" had turned into a relentless pursuit of perfection.

Aaron had warned her about this.

"Minimalism isn't about doing more with less," he had said over coffee one afternoon. "It's about doing less with more intention. It's easy to get caught up in the idea of being productive and efficient, but at its core, minimalism is about finding balance and joy in simplicity."

Emily had nodded, agreeing with him at the time. But now, as she sat amidst her self-imposed chaos, she realized she had missed the point entirely. Her well-intentioned efforts to simplify had spiraled into an exhausting cycle of overcommitment, leaving her burnt out and disillusioned.

The realization hit her like a wave, washing over her with a mixture of guilt and disappointment. She felt like a failure, like she wasn't "doing" minimalism correctly. The pressure to succeed, even in simplifying her life, was overwhelming.

She needed help.

With a sigh, Emily closed her laptop and grabbed her phone. She hesitated for a moment, then scrolled through her contacts and dialed Aaron's number. It rang twice before he picked up.

"Hey, Emily! What's up?" Aaron's voice was cheerful, as always.

Emily hesitated, unsure how to start. "Hey, Aaron. I... I think I need some advice."

"Of course. What's going on?"

"I'm feeling overwhelmed," Emily admitted, her voice cracking slightly. "I thought I was doing everything right—decluttering, saying no to things that don't matter, focusing on my priorities—but it's all just too much. I'm exhausted, and I don't know what to do."

Aaron was silent for a moment, letting her words sink in. "I hear you, Emily. It sounds like you're experiencing burnout."

"Yeah," Emily sighed. "I think I am. But how is that possible? I thought minimalism was supposed to make life easier, not harder."

"It is," Aaron agreed. "But it's easy to fall into the trap of trying to 'do' minimalism perfectly. Remember, it's not about being perfect. It's about being intentional. And sometimes, that means stepping back and re-evaluating what's important to you."

Emily nodded, even though he couldn't see her. "So, what do I do?"

"First things first," Aaron said gently. "Give yourself permission to rest. You've been pushing yourself too hard, and you need to recharge. Take a break from your commitments, even if it's just for a day or two. And then, when you're feeling more grounded, we can talk about how to move forward."

Emily felt a wave of relief wash over her. "Thanks, Aaron. I appreciate it."

"Anytime, Emily. Remember, you're not alone in this. We all go through ups and downs on our minimalist journey. It's all part of the process."

They said their goodbyes, and Emily hung up the phone, feeling a little lighter. She took Aaron's advice to heart, deciding to take a break from her responsibilities. For the first time in weeks, she allowed herself to relax, to simply be.

The next day, Emily woke up with a sense of determination. She was still tired, but there was a newfound clarity in her mind. She spent the morning in quiet reflection, sipping tea on her balcony and watching the city come to life below.

As the day went on, she found herself drawn to her journal, a gift from Aaron when she first began her minimalist journey. She hadn't written in it for weeks, too caught up in the hustle of daily life. Now, she opened it to a blank page and began to write.

Dear Emily,

I know you're feeling overwhelmed right now. You've been trying so hard to live a meaningful, intentional life, and that's not easy. It's okay to feel tired. It's okay to feel lost.

You're doing the best you can, and that's enough.

Remember why you started this journey. It wasn't to impress anyone or to prove that you could live with less. It was to find peace, to focus on what truly matters to you.

Take a deep breath. Let go of the pressure to be perfect. It's okay to rest. It's okay to take things slow. You've got this.

Love, Emily

As she wrote, Emily felt a sense of calm wash over her. The act of putting her thoughts and feelings on paper was cathartic, helping her process the emotions she had been bottling up. She realized that she had been too hard on herself, expecting perfection in a journey that was never meant to be about perfection.

Minimalism wasn't a competition. It was a personal journey, unique to each individual. And right now, her journey required her to slow down, to rest, and to find joy in simplicity once more.

Over the next few days, Emily focused on self-care. She spent time meditating, practicing yoga, and taking long walks in the park. She disconnected from her phone, setting boundaries for digital use and allowing herself to be present in the moment.

As she walked through the park one sunny afternoon, Emily noticed the vibrant colors of the changing leaves, the crispness of the autumn air, and the sound of children laughing in the distance. She felt a sense of peace that had eluded her for weeks, a reminder of the beauty in simple moments.

She realized that she had been so focused on decluttering her physical space and managing her responsibilities that she had forgotten to declutter her mind and soul. She needed to let go of the guilt, the pressure, and the expectations she had placed on herself.

After her walk, Emily sat on a bench and took out her journal once more. She began to write down the things that truly mattered to her, the core values that had guided her minimalist journey from the start:

Connection – Building meaningful relationships with loved ones.Growth – Continuously learning and evolving as a person.Presence – Being mindful and fully engaged in the moment.Joy – Finding happiness in simple pleasures and experiences.Purpose – Living a life aligned with her passions and values.

As she wrote, Emily felt a renewed sense of clarity. These were the things that mattered to her, the reasons she had embraced minimalism in the first place. They weren't about achieving perfection or keeping up with a minimalist ideal. They were about living a life that felt authentic and fulfilling.

With this newfound perspective, Emily decided to make some changes. She realized that she needed to set clearer boundaries and prioritize her own well-being. She couldn't do everything, and that was okay. It was time to let go of the commitments that no longer served her and focus on what truly mattered.

The following week, Emily took action. She reached out to her colleagues and explained that she needed to scale back her workload. She delegated tasks where she could and set realistic expectations for herself. It wasn't easy, but she knew it was necessary for her own well-being.

She also stepped down from organizing the minimalist meet-ups, passing the baton to someone else in the community who was eager to take on the role. It was a bittersweet decision, but Emily knew she needed to prioritize her time and energy.

With fewer commitments, Emily found herself with more time to breathe, to relax, and to enjoy the simple pleasures in life. She reconnected with friends she hadn't seen in months, spending lazy afternoons in coffee shops, laughing and sharing stories.

She also made time for herself, indulging in her favorite hobbies like reading, painting, and cooking. She found joy in the little things, like the smell of fresh coffee in the morning or the feel of a soft blanket on a chilly evening.

Through it all, Emily learned to be kinder to herself. She realized that burnout was not a sign of failure but a reminder to slow down and listen to her own needs. Minimalism wasn't a race; it was a journey of self-discovery and growth.

As the days passed, Emily felt a renewed sense of purpose. She was still committed to living a minimalist life, but now she understood that it wasn't about having less or doing more. It was about finding balance, being present, and living with intention.

She knew there would be challenges ahead, moments of doubt and uncertainty. But she also knew that she was capable of overcoming them. With each step she took, she was learning, growing, and becoming more in tune with herself.

One evening, as she sat on her balcony watching the sunset, Emily felt a deep sense of contentment. The sky was painted in hues of orange and pink, and the city below buzzed with life. She took a deep breath, savoring the moment.

She thought back to the beginning of her minimalist journey, when she had first decided to let go of the excess and embrace a simpler life. She had come so far since then, learning valuable lessons along the way.

Burnout had been a wake-up call, a reminder that she needed to take care of herself and prioritize her own well-being. It had taught her the importance of setting boundaries, of saying no when necessary, and of being true to her own needs and values.

Emily smiled, feeling a sense of gratitude for the journey she was on. It wasn't always easy, but it was hers. And for that, she was thankful.

# Chapter 16: Breaking Habits

Emily woke up to the sound of her alarm buzzing incessantly on her nightstand. She rolled over, groggily fumbling to silence it. The early morning light filtered through the thin curtains of her new, smaller apartment, casting a soft glow over the minimalist space she had worked so hard to create.

Her closet, once overflowing with clothes, now housed only a few carefully chosen items. Her kitchen, once a mess of mismatched gadgets and rarely used appliances, was now clean and organized. Everything had a place, and for the first time in her life, Emily felt a sense of calm when she looked around her home.

Today was going to be different, she told herself. Today, she was determined to maintain the minimalist habits she had worked so hard to cultivate. She had been reading about the importance of routine and discipline in living a minimalist lifestyle, and she knew that to stay on track, she would need to make a conscious effort to break the old habits that had led her to accumulate so much in the first place.

She sat up in bed, took a deep breath, and stretched her arms over her head. She grabbed her journal from the nightstand and flipped to a fresh page. "Intentions for Today," she wrote at the top, underlining it for emphasis. Below, she listed three simple goals:

Be mindful of spendingLimit social media to 30 minutesFocus on experiences, not things

With her intentions set, Emily closed the journal and got out of bed, feeling a renewed sense of purpose. She quickly got dressed in her favorite pair of jeans and a soft, white t-shirt. She had learned to appreciate the simplicity of a small wardrobe; every piece was something she loved, something that made her feel good. There was no more agonizing over what to wear – just a quick decision, and she was ready to go.

Emily walked into the kitchen and made herself a cup of coffee, savoring the rich aroma as it filled the room. As she sipped her coffee, she glanced at her phone. The urge to scroll through social media was strong – it always was first thing in the morning – but she reminded herself of her goal. She set a timer for 30 minutes, determined not to exceed her limit.

Old Habits Die Hard

The morning passed quickly. Emily spent a few hours working on a project for her job, losing herself in the creative process. It felt good to be productive, to focus on something meaningful instead of wasting time on her phone. But as lunchtime approached, Emily started to feel restless.

She decided to take a break and head out for a walk. The sun was shining, and the crisp autumn air was refreshing. She loved the feeling of getting outside, of clearing her mind and reconnecting with nature. It was one of the habits she had picked up on her minimalist journey, and it never failed to lift her spirits.

As she walked through her neighborhood, Emily noticed a new boutique that had just opened. The window display was filled with beautiful, handcrafted jewelry and stylish, minimalist clothing. Emily felt a pang of curiosity. She loved discovering new shops, and the temptation to go inside and take a look was strong.

She paused for a moment, remembering her intention to be mindful of spending. Did she really need anything new? She had spent the past several months carefully curating her wardrobe, making sure each item had a purpose and a place. The last thing she needed was to add more clutter to her life.

But the pull was strong. She reasoned that it wouldn't hurt to just take a look. She wasn't planning on buying anything – just browsing.

Emily stepped inside, and a friendly sales associate greeted her with a warm smile. "Welcome! Feel free to look around," she said. Emily nodded, thanking her, and began to browse the racks.

She picked up a delicate gold necklace, admiring the craftsmanship. It was beautiful, and she could picture it perfectly complementing the simple outfits in her closet. The price tag, however, gave her pause. It was more than she would typically spend on jewelry, especially since she had been trying to cut back on unnecessary purchases.

Still, the urge to buy was there. She could feel the familiar rush of excitement – that brief, fleeting high that came with buying something new. It was a feeling she hadn't experienced in a while, and it was intoxicating.

Emily reminded herself of her commitment to minimalism, her promise to be mindful of her spending. She took a deep breath and put the necklace back on the rack. She could admire its beauty without owning it, she told herself.

But as she continued to browse, she found herself struggling to resist the urge to buy. There was a cozy sweater that looked perfect for the chilly autumn days ahead, a pair of leather boots that would be perfect for work, and a sleek black handbag that caught her eye.

Emily's resolve wavered. She had worked so hard to break these habits, to focus on what truly mattered instead of getting caught up in the cycle of consumption. But here she was, tempted by the allure of new things, just like before.

She took a deep breath, trying to clear her mind. She needed to refocus, to remind herself why she had chosen this path in the first place. She thought about the clutter that had once filled her apartment, the stress and overwhelm that came with owning too much. She remembered the freedom she had felt when she began to let go, the peace that came from simplifying her life.

With a renewed sense of determination, Emily put the sweater back on the rack, the boots back on the shelf, and the handbag back on display. She thanked the sales associate and quickly left the store, feeling a mix of relief and frustration.

The Cycle of Temptation

As Emily walked away from the boutique, she felt a wave of emotions wash over her. She was proud of herself for resisting the temptation to buy, but she was also frustrated that she had been so easily swayed. She had thought she was past this, that she had learned to break these habits once and for all.

She took out her phone and checked the time. Her 30-minute limit for social media had long since passed, but she felt the familiar urge to scroll, to distract herself from the frustration she was feeling. She opened her Instagram app and began to mindlessly scroll through her feed, liking photos of friends and influencers, each one more curated and polished than the last.

As she scrolled, she noticed an ad for a sale at one of her favorite online stores. The timing was uncanny – almost as if her phone knew she was feeling vulnerable, looking for a quick fix. Emily felt the temptation rising again. Maybe she could just take a look, see if there was anything she needed...

She caught herself. What was she doing? She had just resolved to break these habits, to focus on experiences instead of things. Yet here she was, falling back into the same patterns of mindless scrolling and impulsive shopping.

Emily put her phone away and took a deep breath, reminding herself of her intentions for the day. She needed to stay focused, to resist the urge to fall back into old habits. It wasn't easy – breaking habits never was – but she knew it was worth it.

Seeking Guidance

Feeling the need for support, Emily decided to reach out to Aaron, her minimalist mentor. Aaron had been instrumental in guiding her on her journey, offering advice and encouragement whenever she needed it. He had been living a minimalist lifestyle for years and had a way of putting things into perspective.

Emily dialed his number, and after a few rings, he picked up. "Hey, Emily! How's it going?" Aaron's voice was warm and friendly, instantly putting her at ease.

"Hey, Aaron. I'm good, but I'm struggling a bit today," Emily admitted. "I've been trying to stick to my minimalist habits, but I keep getting tempted by old patterns. I almost bought a bunch of stuff at a boutique, and I've already exceeded my social media limit for the day. I just feel like I'm slipping back into old habits, and it's frustrating."

Aaron listened patiently, nodding along as she spoke. "I hear you, Emily. It's completely normal to have days like this, especially when you're trying to break old habits. The important thing is that you're aware of it and that you're trying to make a change."

Emily sighed. "I just feel like I should be further along by now. I've been doing this for months, and I thought I had it all figured out. But today, it feels like I'm back at square one."

Aaron chuckled softly. "Trust me, you're not back at square one. This journey isn't about perfection – it's about progress. Breaking habits takes time, and it's okay to have setbacks. What matters is that you recognize them and keep moving forward."

Emily nodded, taking in his words. "I guess I just need to be more patient with myself. It's just hard sometimes, you know?"

"I know," Aaron said. "But remember, minimalism isn't about depriving yourself or being perfect. It's about finding what truly brings you joy and letting go of the rest. It's a process, and it's different for everyone. The fact that you're aware of your habits and trying to change them is a huge step in the right direction."

Emily felt a sense of relief wash over her. Aaron was right – she needed to be kinder to herself, to recognize that change didn't happen overnight. She thanked him for his support, promising to keep moving forward and stay focused on her goals.

Mindfulness and Forgiveness

After her conversation with Aaron, Emily felt more grounded. She decided to head to a nearby park, a place she often went to clear her mind and find peace. The park was quiet, with only a few people scattered on benches or walking their dogs. Emily found a secluded spot under a large oak tree and sat down, closing her eyes and taking a deep breath.

She focused on her breath, letting each inhale and exhale ground her in the present moment. She had learned about mindfulness on her minimalist journey, and it had become a valuable tool in helping her stay focused and intentional.

As she sat in silence, Emily reflected on her day. She thought about the boutique, the temptation to buy, and the urge to scroll through social media. She realized that these habits were deeply ingrained in her, built up over years of living in a consumer-driven society. They wouldn't disappear overnight, and that was okay.

She needed to forgive herself for slipping up, to recognize that breaking habits was a journey, not a destination. She needed to be patient and compassionate with herself, to allow herself the grace to make mistakes and learn from them.

Emily opened her eyes, feeling a sense of calm wash over her. She had been so focused on doing everything right, on being the perfect minimalist, that she had forgotten the importance of self-compassion. She needed to remember that this journey was about more than just decluttering and reducing; it was about finding peace and contentment within herself.

Recommitting to the Journey

As the sun began to set, casting a warm golden glow over the park, Emily stood up and brushed the leaves off her jeans. She felt a renewed sense of purpose, a commitment to continue her journey with a more mindful and forgiving attitude.

She pulled out her journal and opened to the page where she had written her intentions for the day. She added a fourth goal: 4. Practice self-compassion.

With her journal in hand, Emily made her way home, feeling lighter than she had in weeks. She knew that there would be more challenges ahead, more temptations to fall back into old habits. But she also knew that she had the strength to overcome them, to stay true to her values and live a life of intention.

When she arrived back at her apartment, she made herself a simple dinner and sat down at her small, wooden dining table. She savored each bite, appreciating the simplicity of the meal and the calm of her surroundings. She didn't need anything more than this – just good food, a peaceful home, and the knowledge that she was on the right path.

After dinner, Emily decided to wind down with a book. She had been making an effort to read more, to fill her time with activities that nourished her soul instead of numbing her mind. She chose a book on mindfulness, curling up on the couch with a cozy blanket.

As she read, she felt a sense of contentment wash over her. She was learning to break old habits, to let go of what no longer served her, and to focus on what truly mattered. It wasn't always easy, but it was worth it.

Emily closed her book and set it on the coffee table, feeling a sense of gratitude for the journey she was on. She had come a long way since she first discovered minimalism, and she knew she still had a long way to go. But for the first time in a long time, she felt at peace with where she was and excited for what lay ahead.

She turned off the lights and headed to bed, feeling a sense of calm wash over her. She knew that tomorrow would bring new challenges, new temptations to fall back into old habits. But she also knew that she had the tools and the strength to overcome them.

Emily climbed into bed, pulling the covers up to her chin. She took a deep breath, closing her eyes and letting the day's events fade away. She was ready for whatever came next, ready to continue her journey with a renewed sense of purpose and a commitment to living a life of intention.

As she drifted off to sleep, Emily felt a sense of peace settle over her. She knew that breaking habits wasn't easy, but she also knew that it was worth it. She was on the right path, and she was determined to keep moving forward, one step at a time.

# Chapter 17: Navigating Relationships

Emily sat at her kitchen table, staring blankly at her phone. The screen glowed with a message from her longtime friend, Jessica, who had been her closest confidante since college. They had seen each other through heartbreaks, career changes, and countless late-night conversations over wine and laughter. But recently, their friendship had begun to feel strained. Jessica's message was brief, just a question about meeting up for lunch. But Emily hesitated to respond, feeling a knot tighten in her stomach.

It wasn't the first time Emily had felt this way. Since adopting her minimalist lifestyle, she had started to notice changes in all her relationships. The more she decluttered her life, the more she realized how much of it had been filled with people, obligations, and expectations that no longer aligned with who she was becoming. She had hoped her friendships would withstand these changes, but now she wasn't so sure.

Emily took a deep breath, tapping out a quick reply agreeing to lunch. As she hit send, she resolved to use the opportunity to finally talk to Jessica about what she had been feeling. She knew it wouldn't be easy, but she also knew it was necessary.

The next day, Emily arrived at their usual café, a cozy spot with mismatched furniture and an inviting atmosphere. She spotted Jessica at a corner table, waving her over with a bright smile. As Emily approached, she took a moment to observe her friend. Jessica looked the same as always: impeccably dressed in the latest fashion, her hair perfectly styled. She radiated an effortless confidence that Emily had always admired.

"Hey, you!" Jessica exclaimed, pulling Emily into a hug. "It's been too long. How have you been?"

"I've been... good," Emily replied, sliding into the seat across from Jessica. She forced a smile, trying to push down the nervous flutter in her stomach. "Just busy with work and... life stuff."

"I hear you," Jessica said, rolling her eyes. "Work has been insane for me too. Honestly, I've been dying for a break. We should plan a girls' trip soon, don't you think? Like old times?"

Emily hesitated, the knot in her stomach tightening. "Actually, Jess, there's something I've been meaning to talk to you about."

Jessica's smile faltered slightly, her eyes narrowing with curiosity. "Okay, what's up?"

Emily took a deep breath, her hands fidgeting with the edge of her napkin. "I've been thinking a lot about my life lately, about what I want and what really matters to me. And I've realized that I need to make some changes."

Jessica's eyebrows shot up. "Changes? Like what?"

"Like how I spend my time, who I spend it with," Emily said, choosing her words carefully. "Since I started embracing minimalism, I've been trying to focus more on what brings me joy and meaning. And I've realized that some of the things I used to prioritize don't really align with that anymore."

Jessica leaned back in her chair, crossing her arms. "And you're saying I'm one of those things?"

"No, Jess, that's not what I mean," Emily said quickly, shaking her head. "I value our friendship, I really do. But I feel like... I don't know, like we've been drifting apart. We're in different places now, and sometimes I feel like we're just going through the motions, you know?"

Jessica's face softened, but her eyes held a hint of hurt. "I didn't realize you felt that way. I thought we were fine."

"I thought so too, at first," Emily admitted. "But then I started to notice how drained I felt after we hung out, like I was trying to be someone I'm not anymore. And it's not just with you—it's with a lot of people in my life. I'm trying to figure out who I am now and what kind of relationships I want to have."

Jessica was silent for a moment, her gaze dropping to the table. When she finally spoke, her voice was quiet. "I guess I didn't realize things had changed so much for you. I've noticed you've been different lately, but I thought it was just a phase or something."

"It's more than that," Emily said softly. "I'm trying to live with more intention, to focus on what really matters to me. And I want my friendships to reflect that too."

Jessica nodded slowly, her expression thoughtful. "I get that. I mean, I don't really understand this whole minimalist thing, but I get wanting to live with purpose. I just... I don't want to lose you, Em. You've been my best friend for so long, and I don't know what I'd do without you."

Emily felt a pang of guilt, but she pushed it aside, knowing she needed to be honest. "I don't want to lose you either, Jess. But I also don't want to keep pretending everything is the same when it's not. I want us to be real with each other, even if that means having some tough conversations."

Jessica nodded again, her eyes glistening with unshed tears. "Okay. I can do that. I don't want to pretend either. I want to be there for you, even if I don't fully get what you're going through."

Emily reached across the table, squeezing Jessica's hand. "Thank you. That means a lot to me."

They sat in silence for a moment, holding hands and letting the weight of their words settle between them. Emily felt a sense of relief wash over her, knowing that she had taken a step toward being more authentic in her relationships. It wasn't easy, but it felt right.

Over the next few weeks, Emily continued to navigate the shifting dynamics of her friendships. Some conversations were easier than others, but each one brought her closer to understanding who she was becoming and what she needed from her relationships.

With Jessica, things had been awkward at first. They had both agreed to take some space to process their conversation, and it had been weeks since they last saw each other. Emily missed her friend but knew that the distance was necessary for both of them to grow.

One evening, as Emily was sitting on her balcony with a cup of tea, her phone buzzed with a new message. She glanced at the screen and saw a text from Jessica.

Jessica: "Hey, I've been thinking a lot about what you said. I'd love to catch up and talk more. Are you free this weekend?"

Emily smiled, her heart lifting at the sight of Jessica's message. She quickly typed out a response, agreeing to meet up. As she set her phone down, she felt a sense of gratitude for the opportunity to reconnect on a deeper level.

When Saturday arrived, Emily found herself back at the same café, nervously waiting for Jessica to arrive. She had spent the past few days reflecting on their friendship, trying to figure out what she wanted to say.

A few minutes later, Jessica walked in, looking more relaxed than Emily had seen her in a long time. She waved at Emily and made her way over, a tentative smile on her face.

"Hey," Jessica said as she sat down. "Thanks for meeting me."

"Of course," Emily replied, returning the smile. "I'm glad you reached out."

Jessica took a deep breath, her expression serious. "I've been doing a lot of thinking since we last talked. And I realized that you're right. We have been drifting apart, and I think part of it is because I've been holding on to this idea of who you used to be instead of accepting who you are now."

Emily felt a lump form in her throat, touched by Jessica's honesty. "That means a lot to me, Jess. I know it's not easy to accept change, especially when it feels like you're losing something."

"I don't want to lose you," Jessica said firmly. "I want to understand this new version of you, even if it means letting go of the past. I want to be the kind of friend you need, not just the friend I've always been."

Emily felt tears prick at the corners of her eyes. "Thank you. That's all I've ever wanted. I don't expect you to change who you are, but I appreciate you being willing to meet me where I am."

Jessica nodded, a small smile tugging at her lips. "So, tell me more about this minimalism thing. I want to understand what it means to you and how it's changed your life."

Emily spent the next hour sharing her journey with Jessica, explaining how minimalism had helped her find clarity and purpose. She talked about the joy she felt in letting go of excess and the freedom she had found in living with intention.

Jessica listened intently, asking questions and nodding along. As Emily spoke, she felt a renewed sense of connection with her friend, a reminder that their bond was deeper than their differences.

By the time they left the café, Emily felt lighter, knowing that she and Jessica were on a path to rebuilding their friendship with honesty and mutual understanding. It wasn't a perfect resolution, but it was a start—a step toward navigating their relationship with intention and authenticity.

As Emily continued her journey, she found herself reassessing other relationships in her life as well. She began to recognize which friendships truly nurtured her and which ones felt like obligations or habits. She started to distance herself from people who drained her energy, focusing instead on deepening her connections with those who supported her growth.

One of those people was Aaron, her mentor and friend who had introduced her to minimalism. They had developed a close bond over the past few months, sharing countless conversations about life, philosophy, and the pursuit of simplicity. Aaron had become a steady presence in Emily's life, offering guidance and encouragement whenever she needed it.

One evening, after a particularly challenging day at work, Emily decided to call Aaron. She felt a wave of relief when he answered on the first ring.

"Hey, Emily," Aaron said, his voice warm and reassuring. "How are you doing?"

"I've been better," Emily admitted, leaning back against her couch. "I had a rough day at work, and I've just been feeling... overwhelmed. Like I'm still trying to figure out who I am and what I want from my relationships."

Aaron was silent for a moment, then spoke thoughtfully. "That's a tough place to be, but it's also a necessary part of the journey. Growth is uncomfortable, especially when it means reevaluating the people we've surrounded ourselves with. But it's also a sign that you're moving in the right direction."

Emily nodded, even though Aaron couldn't see her. "I know. It's just hard to let go of people, even when you know it's for the best. I've been struggling with that a lot lately."

"It's natural to feel that way," Aaron said gently. "But remember, minimalism isn't just about letting go of physical things. It's also about clearing space in your life for what truly matters. Sometimes that means letting go of relationships that no longer serve you, so you can make room for the ones that do."

Emily sighed, feeling a mixture of relief and sadness. "I know you're right. It's just... I've been friends with some of these people for so long. It feels like I'm losing a part of myself."

"You're not losing anything," Aaron said firmly. "You're evolving. And as you evolve, so will your relationships. Some will grow with you, and others won't. That's just a part of life. The important thing is to stay true to yourself and to surround yourself with people who support and uplift you."

Emily smiled, grateful for Aaron's wisdom. "Thank you, Aaron. You always know just what to say."

"I'm glad I could help," Aaron replied. "And remember, you're not alone in this. I'm here for you, and so are the people who truly care about you."

Emily felt a warmth spread through her chest, knowing that Aaron was right. She wasn't alone. She had people in her life who understood her, who supported her, and who wanted to see her thrive.

As she hung up the phone, Emily felt a renewed sense of clarity. She knew that navigating her relationships would continue to be a challenge, but she also knew that she was on the right path. By living with intention and authenticity, she was creating a life filled with meaningful connections and genuine support.

And that was worth all the difficult conversations in the world.

A few days later, Emily found herself at a dinner party hosted by one of her colleagues. She had been hesitant to attend, knowing that many of the guests were people she hadn't seen in months—people she had intentionally distanced herself from as she embraced her minimalist lifestyle. But she also knew that she couldn't avoid these encounters forever, and she was determined to face them with grace and authenticity.

As she entered the bustling living room, Emily took a deep breath, scanning the crowd for familiar faces. She spotted a few friends chatting by the bar and made her way over, smiling as she approached.

"Emily! It's so good to see you," one of her friends, Rachel, exclaimed, pulling her into a hug. "We've missed you at these gatherings. Where have you been hiding?"

Emily chuckled, feeling a bit awkward but trying to stay calm. "I've been around, just focusing on some personal stuff. Trying to live a bit more intentionally, you know?"

Rachel nodded, though her expression was puzzled. "Intentionally? Like, how?"

"Well, I've been exploring minimalism," Emily explained. "It's all about simplifying your life, letting go of what doesn't add value, and focusing on what truly matters."

One of the other friends, Ben, raised an eyebrow. "So, you're like getting rid of all your stuff?"

"Sort of," Emily said, choosing her words carefully. "It's not just about getting rid of things. It's about making space for what's important, whether that's in your home, your schedule, or your relationships."

Rachel's eyes widened. "That sounds... intense. I mean, I get wanting to declutter, but it sounds like you're taking it to a whole new level."

Emily smiled, appreciating Rachel's candidness. "It can seem intense, but it's actually been really freeing. I've found so much clarity and peace by simplifying my life. It's helped me focus on what truly makes me happy."

Ben nodded slowly. "I can respect that. It's not for everyone, but if it works for you, more power to you."

Emily felt a wave of relief wash over her. She had been worried about how her friends would react to her new lifestyle, but their openness and curiosity were reassuring.

As the night went on, Emily found herself engaged in deeper conversations with her friends, sharing more about her journey and listening to their own experiences. She realized that while not everyone would understand or embrace minimalism, many of them were supportive and willing to learn.

By the end of the evening, Emily felt a sense of contentment she hadn't expected. She had navigated a potentially uncomfortable situation with honesty and grace, staying true to herself while remaining open to others. It was a reminder that her relationships, like her life, could be both simple and meaningful if she approached them with intention.

# Chapter 18: The Cost of Less

Emily stared at her bank account statement, a sinking feeling in her stomach. The numbers didn't lie—she was running out of money. Her minimalist lifestyle, which had brought her so much clarity and peace, was now confronting her with a harsh reality. Living with less wasn't just about fewer possessions; it also meant grappling with the financial implications of her choices.

It all started when Emily decided to quit her high-stress corporate job. The decision wasn't made lightly. For years, she had felt trapped in a cycle of overwork, consumerism, and constant anxiety. The minimalist philosophy had given her the courage to reassess her priorities, leading her to pursue a simpler, more meaningful life. She had taken a part-time job at a local bookstore, a place that aligned with her values and allowed her the freedom to live at a slower pace. But with that choice came a significant reduction in income.

At first, the adjustment felt liberating. Emily reveled in the newfound time and mental space. She spent her days reading, writing, and exploring her city with fresh eyes. She no longer felt the need to buy things to fill a void, and her expenses had drastically decreased. Gone were the splurges on designer clothes, expensive dinners, and unnecessary gadgets. She had embraced the minimalist mantra: less is more.

But now, six months later, the financial strain was beginning to show. Emily's savings were dwindling, and unexpected expenses had started to pile up. Her old car, which she had decided to keep rather than replace with a new one, needed a costly repair. Her rent, though reasonable for her city, was still a significant monthly burden. And then there were the medical bills—a sudden reminder that health problems don't care about your minimalist ideals.

Emily had always believed that by living simply, she could live more affordably. But she was beginning to realize that minimalism didn't automatically equate to financial stability. The cost of living, even when stripped down to the essentials, was still significant. And without the safety net of a high-paying job, every financial hit felt like a blow to her carefully constructed life.

She found herself at a crossroads. Should she return to the corporate world, with its promise of financial security but at the cost of her mental well-being? Or should she find another way to make minimalism financially sustainable?

Understanding Financial Minimalism

Emily decided to seek advice from Aaron, her minimalist mentor who had guided her through so many challenges on this journey. Aaron had always seemed to live effortlessly within his means, balancing his minimalist values with a pragmatic approach to finances. She hoped he could offer some guidance.

Over coffee in a small, cozy café, Emily poured out her worries to Aaron. She talked about her dwindling savings, her fear of financial insecurity, and the guilt she felt for not being able to make minimalism work financially.

Aaron listened carefully, nodding in understanding. "Emily," he began, "minimalism is not a magic solution to all of life's problems, especially when it comes to money. It's about aligning your life with your values, yes, but it also requires careful planning and a realistic approach to finances."

He paused, taking a sip of his coffee before continuing. "There's a concept called financial minimalism, which is about managing your money in a way that supports your minimalist lifestyle. It's not just about spending less, but about making conscious decisions with your money—understanding your needs versus your wants, planning for the future, and being prepared for the unexpected."

Emily nodded slowly, absorbing his words. She realized that in her excitement to embrace a simpler life, she had overlooked the need to adapt her financial habits to her new lifestyle.

The Reality of Fixed Costs

Aaron continued, "One of the biggest challenges in financial minimalism is dealing with fixed costs—the expenses you can't easily reduce or eliminate. Rent, utilities, transportation, health insurance—these are all essential, but they can add up quickly. The key is to find a balance between living simply and ensuring that you can cover these costs without stress."

Emily thought about her own fixed costs. Her rent was the largest expense, followed by her car and insurance. She had already cut back on utilities by being mindful of her energy use, and she rarely ate out anymore. But the car repair had been an unexpected blow, and she knew she couldn't afford another surprise like that.

"I've been thinking about moving to a smaller place," Emily admitted. "Something cheaper, maybe even a shared living situation. But I'm worried about giving up my independence."

Aaron smiled gently. "It's a trade-off, like so many things in life. Moving to a smaller place or sharing living expenses with someone else could free up a significant portion of your budget. But it's important to weigh that against the value you place on your current living situation. What does your space give you that you might lose in a smaller or shared place?"

Emily considered this. Her apartment, though modest, was her sanctuary. It was where she had created her minimalist home, a place that reflected her journey and brought her peace. Moving to a cheaper place would mean more financial security, but it could also mean sacrificing the comfort and stability she had built.

"I'm not saying you should move," Aaron clarified. "But if you're serious about making minimalism work financially, it's worth exploring all your options. Sometimes, downsizing can lead to unexpected benefits—less space means less to maintain, fewer things to clean, and more money for experiences or savings."

Creative Solutions and New Opportunities

Over the next few weeks, Emily began to explore ways to reduce her expenses and increase her income without compromising her minimalist values. She started by revisiting her budget, identifying areas where she could cut back even further. She cancelled subscriptions she rarely used, renegotiated her phone plan, and found cheaper alternatives for some of her essential purchases.

But she knew that cutting costs alone wouldn't be enough. She needed to find a way to bring in more income, preferably through something that aligned with her minimalist philosophy.

One day, as she was browsing through the bookstore where she worked, Emily stumbled upon a book about freelancing and the gig economy. The idea intrigued her. She had always enjoyed writing and had even started a blog about her minimalist journey. Maybe, she thought, she could turn her passion for writing into a source of income.

She began researching freelance writing opportunities, learning about different platforms where she could offer her services. She also reached out to her network, letting friends and former colleagues know that she was available for freelance work. Within a few weeks, she had landed her first writing gig—an article about the benefits of minimalist living for a lifestyle website.

The extra income from freelancing wasn't huge, but it was enough to ease some of the financial pressure. More importantly, it gave Emily a sense of empowerment. She was taking control of her financial situation in a way that didn't compromise her values. By leveraging her skills and passions, she was creating a more sustainable minimalist lifestyle.

Facing the Unexpected

Just as Emily began to feel more confident about her financial situation, life threw her another curveball. One morning, she woke up with a severe toothache. A visit to the dentist confirmed her worst fear: she needed a root canal, and it wasn't going to be cheap.

The news hit Emily hard. She had been so careful with her budget, so diligent about saving every penny she could. But no amount of planning could have prepared her for this unexpected expense. As she sat in the dentist's office, discussing payment options, she felt a wave of frustration and despair. How was she supposed to pay for this? Wasn't minimalism supposed to protect her from this kind of stress?

She reached out to Aaron again, hoping for some guidance. "I thought I had everything under control," she admitted, her voice heavy with frustration. "But now this happens, and I feel like all my efforts have been for nothing."

Aaron listened patiently. "Emily, I understand how you feel. But remember, minimalism isn't about eliminating all challenges from your life. It's about simplifying and focusing on what truly matters. And sometimes, what matters is taking care of yourself, even if it means spending money you didn't plan to spend."

He continued, "Unexpected expenses are a part of life, whether you're a minimalist or not. The difference is in how you approach them. Instead of seeing this as a failure, try to view it as an opportunity to reassess and adjust your approach. Maybe it's time to start building a stronger emergency fund, or to explore more ways to increase your income."

Redefining Success

After her conversation with Aaron, Emily took a step back to reevaluate her situation. She realized that her frustration wasn't just about the cost of the root canal—it was also about the unrealistic expectations she had set for herself. She had believed that by embracing minimalism, she could avoid all financial stress and live a perfectly balanced life. But life, she now understood, didn't work that way.

Minimalism had given her many tools to simplify and focus on what truly mattered, but it wasn't a cure-all. It didn't protect her from unexpected expenses, health issues, or the ups and downs of life. What it did offer, however, was a framework for dealing with these challenges in a more intentional way.

Emily decided to adjust her mindset. Instead of seeing financial setbacks as failures, she would view them as part of the journey—lessons to be learned and opportunities to grow. She began setting aside a small portion of her freelance income for an emergency fund, slowly rebuilding her financial safety net. She also continued to explore new ways to increase her income, from expanding her freelance work to exploring passive income streams.

Finding Balance

As the months passed, Emily's financial situation gradually stabilized. The combination of careful budgeting, increased income, and a stronger emergency fund gave her a sense of security she hadn't felt in a long time. She no longer feared the unexpected; instead, she felt prepared to face whatever challenges came her way.

But more importantly, Emily found a new sense of balance. She realized that minimalism wasn't about living with as little as possible or avoiding all financial challenges. It was about aligning her life with her values, making conscious choices, and finding contentment in the simple things.

She learned to appreciate the benefits of her minimalist lifestyle, even when faced with financial stress. The freedom of living with less allowed her to focus on experiences rather than possessions. She found joy in the little things—reading a good book, spending time with friends, exploring nature. These moments, she realized, were priceless, far more valuable than any material possession.

# Chapter 19: A Minimalist Home

Emily stood in the doorway of her apartment, surveying the familiar space that had been her home for the last five years. It was a sunny Saturday afternoon, and the light streamed through the large windows, casting a warm glow on the room. She was struck by how much had changed in this space since she first moved in.

When she arrived, fresh out of college and eager to start her career, the apartment had been a blank slate—an empty canvas waiting to be filled with the trappings of her new life. She had quickly set about doing just that. Over the years, she filled the space with stylish furniture, wall art, trinkets, books, and more. Every corner of the apartment held something she thought she needed to complete her life or impress others.

But now, standing in the middle of it all, Emily felt a deep sense of disconnection from these things. They no longer represented her or the life she wanted. After months of embracing minimalism, she had begun to see her possessions differently. Instead of bringing joy, they felt like anchors, tethering her to a past that no longer resonated with who she was.

Emily's journey toward a minimalist lifestyle had been gradual but transformative. She started by decluttering her closet, then moved on to other areas of her home, and even tackled her digital life. Each step brought her a sense of lightness and clarity she hadn't felt in years. But now, she wanted to take the next big step—downsizing her living space.

The decision hadn't come easily. Emily loved her apartment. It was spacious, bright, and conveniently located. But it also felt excessive for one person, especially one committed to living with less. She often found herself walking through rooms she barely used, cleaning spaces that didn't need to be maintained, and paying for utilities and rent that far exceeded her needs. She realized that living in a large apartment contradicted the minimalist principles she had come to value.

The idea of downsizing excited her. It represented a new chapter, a way to fully embrace her minimalist philosophy. She wanted to create a home that reflected her values—a space that was simple, intentional, and free of unnecessary clutter. She imagined a place where every item had a purpose and every corner served a function, a space that allowed her to live freely and authentically.

After weeks of searching, she found the perfect place: a small one-bedroom apartment in a quiet neighborhood, just a short walk from a beautiful park. It was half the size of her current apartment, but it was cozy and bright, with just enough space for what she needed. The moment she stepped inside, she felt a sense of calm wash over her. This was it—her new home.

Now, standing in her old apartment, Emily felt a mix of emotions. She was excited about the change, but she was also overwhelmed by the task ahead. Moving was never easy, and moving into a smaller space meant making tough decisions about what to keep and what to let go of.

She took a deep breath and decided to start with the living room. This was the heart of her home, the place where she had spent countless hours with friends, hosting dinners, watching movies, and simply relaxing. She wanted to be intentional about what she brought with her into her new space.

Emily began by assessing her furniture. Her large sectional sofa, though comfortable and perfect for entertaining, would be too big for the new apartment. She decided to sell it and instead keep the smaller armchair, which was cozy and perfect for curling up with a book. The coffee table, with its heavy wood and ornate design, also felt out of place in her new minimalist vision. She opted to donate it and use a simple, sleek side table instead.

As she continued to sort through her things, she came across a stack of photo albums on a shelf. She smiled as she flipped through the pages, remembering the memories captured in each picture. But she realized that she rarely looked at them. They mostly sat on the shelf, gathering dust. She decided to digitize the photos and store them in a cloud, allowing her to access them anytime without the need for physical space.

Next, Emily moved to the kitchen. She loved cooking and had accumulated a wide array of gadgets and appliances over the years—many of which she rarely used. She pulled everything out of the cabinets and drawers and laid it on the counter. The sheer volume of stuff was overwhelming: multiple sets of measuring cups, several spatulas, a pasta maker she had used only once, and countless mismatched Tupperware.

She started by identifying the essentials—the things she used daily or brought her joy. A set of quality knives, a cast iron skillet, a French press, and her favorite ceramic mugs made the cut. The rest, she decided, could go. She donated the excess kitchenware to a local shelter, knowing it would be put to good use.

The bedroom was next. This space had always been a sanctuary for Emily, but she realized it had become cluttered over time. Her dresser was overflowing with clothes, and her nightstand was covered in books she had meant to read but never got around to. She opened her closet and sighed at the sight of clothes she hadn't worn in months.

Emily decided to apply the same principles she used when she first started decluttering her wardrobe. She pulled out each item and asked herself if it was something she loved or wore regularly. If the answer was no, it went into a donation pile. By the time she finished, she had reduced her wardrobe by half, keeping only the pieces that truly fit her style and lifestyle.

She also tackled her bookshelves, which were filled with novels, memoirs, and cookbooks. As an avid reader, this was a tough area for her. But she reminded herself of the joy she felt when she let go of things that no longer served her. She kept only her favorites—books that had profoundly impacted her and ones she knew she would return to. The rest, she donated to a local library.

With each room she tackled, Emily felt a sense of relief. She was shedding layers of her old life, making space for new experiences and opportunities. The process was not just about letting go of physical possessions but also about releasing the emotional baggage tied to them. She felt lighter, freer, and more in control of her life.

As she packed up the last of her things, Emily reflected on the journey that had brought her to this point. Embracing minimalism had been a transformative experience. It had taught her to value experiences over possessions, to seek joy in simplicity, and to live intentionally. She realized that her home was not just a place to store her things but a reflection of her values and priorities.

Finally, moving day arrived. Emily had enlisted the help of a few close friends, who were both supportive and curious about her decision to downsize. They spent the morning loading the moving van with the carefully curated items she had chosen to bring with her.

As they carried the last box out of her old apartment, Emily took one final look around. The once-cluttered space was now empty, its walls bare and its floors clear. She felt a pang of nostalgia but also a sense of closure. This chapter of her life was ending, but she was ready to start a new one.

The drive to her new apartment was short but felt like a journey to a different world. When they arrived, Emily felt a rush of excitement as she unlocked the door and stepped inside. The empty space was a blank canvas, ready to be filled with intention and care.

Her friends helped her unpack, and by the end of the day, the new apartment was starting to feel like home. The furniture fit perfectly, and the minimalist decor created a sense of calm and serenity. Every item had a place and a purpose, and there was plenty of room to breathe.

As they sat on the floor, enjoying takeout pizza and celebrating the successful move, Emily felt a deep sense of contentment. Her new home was everything she had hoped for—simple, cozy, and aligned with her values. She realized that by letting go of excess, she had made space for what truly mattered.

Over the next few weeks, Emily settled into her new space. She took the time to arrange her furniture thoughtfully, placing each piece with intention. She hung a few favorite pieces of art on the walls but kept the overall aesthetic clean and uncluttered. She added a few plants to bring life and color to the space, enjoying the way they made her feel connected to nature.

She also created a small meditation corner, with a cushion and a few candles, where she could start her mornings with mindfulness and gratitude. It was a simple setup, but it brought her immense joy and helped her start each day with a clear and focused mind.

Living in a smaller space required some adjustments, but Emily found that she enjoyed the simplicity. With fewer things to manage and clean, she had more time to focus on what truly mattered to her. She spent more time reading, journaling, and exploring her neighborhood. She discovered new cafes, parks, and community events she had never noticed before.

She also found that her relationships improved. With less space for material distractions, she was more present and engaged with the people in her life. She hosted intimate dinners with close friends, enjoying meaningful conversations and laughter. Her home became a place of connection and joy rather than just a storage space for things.

As Emily continued to embrace her minimalist lifestyle, she found herself drawn to sustainability and mindful consumption. She became more conscious of her impact on the environment and made an effort to reduce waste and live more sustainably. She started composting, using reusable bags and containers, and supporting local, eco-friendly businesses. She realized that minimalism and sustainability went hand in hand, and she was eager to align her lifestyle with her values.

One evening, as Emily sat in her living room, sipping tea and listening to the sounds of the city outside, she reflected on how much her life had changed. Downsizing her home had been a significant step in her minimalist journey, but it was just one part of a larger transformation. She had learned to live with intention, to prioritize what truly mattered, and to find joy in simplicity.

Emily knew that her journey was far from over. Minimalism was not a destination but a continuous process of learning, growing, and evolving. She was excited to see where this path would take her and what new insights and experiences it would bring.

For now, she was content to sit in her cozy, minimalist home, surrounded by the things that truly mattered—a space that reflected her values, nurtured her soul, and allowed her to live fully and authentically.

As she sipped her tea and watched the sunset from her window, Emily smiled, feeling a deep sense of peace and gratitude. She had found her home—not just a physical space but a state of mind, a way of being. And in that moment, she knew that she was exactly where she was meant to be.

# Chapter 20: Creating Space for Growth

Emily stood in the middle of her new apartment, feeling a sense of peace that she hadn't experienced in years. The sunlight streamed through the large windows, casting warm patterns on the freshly painted white walls. The space was much smaller than her old apartment, but it felt expansive. It felt right.

Gone were the cluttered corners, the overstuffed closets, and the oppressive weight of too many things. In their place was a clean, open space with only the essentials: a small couch, a bed, a table with two chairs, and a few carefully chosen decorations that brought her joy. Her heart swelled with contentment as she looked around, knowing that this place was hers—a reflection of the new life she was building.

For months, Emily had been on a journey of transformation. She had let go of more than just physical belongings; she had released old habits, outdated beliefs, and relationships that no longer served her. In their absence, she had found room to breathe, to think, and to grow. Her life had become simpler, but it was also richer, filled with purpose and meaning.

As she continued to unpack the last of her boxes, Emily reflected on how far she had come. Minimalism had started as an experiment, a way to declutter her home and reduce stress. But it had grown into something much deeper—a way of living that prioritized intention and mindfulness. Every choice she made now, from the clothes she wore to the people she spent time with, was guided by her core values.

Moving into this new, smaller apartment was the latest step in her journey. Downsizing had been a difficult decision, but Emily knew it was the right one. Her old apartment, though spacious, had become a symbol of her past—a past filled with excess, distraction, and discontent. She wanted a fresh start, a place where she could fully embrace her new minimalist lifestyle.

With a satisfied sigh, Emily set down the last box and looked around the room. There was still work to be done—pictures to hang, books to arrange, and a few plants to place in the perfect spots. But she didn't feel rushed or overwhelmed. For once, she was content to take her time, to savor each moment as she settled into her new home.

As she moved through the apartment, carefully arranging her belongings, Emily thought about what she wanted to fill this space with. Not more stuff, of course, but experiences, growth, and joy. She wanted this home to be a sanctuary, a place where she could nurture her passions, explore new interests, and continue her journey of self-discovery.

Discovering Meditation

One of the first things Emily decided to add to her new routine was meditation. She had dabbled in it before, but life had always seemed too busy to commit. Now, with fewer distractions and more time on her hands, she felt ready to give it another try.

She cleared a small corner of her living room, placing a soft cushion on the floor and a small plant beside it. It was a simple setup, but it felt serene and inviting. Each morning, she would sit quietly, focusing on her breath and letting her thoughts come and go like passing clouds. At first, it was challenging. Her mind raced with to-do lists, worries, and random thoughts. But slowly, with practice, she began to find a sense of calm and clarity.

Meditation became a cornerstone of her day—a time to reset, to center herself, and to cultivate mindfulness. It helped her stay grounded, even when life got hectic or stressful. It reminded her to be present, to appreciate the small moments, and to live with intention.

Through meditation, Emily also discovered a deeper connection to herself. She learned to listen to her inner voice, to trust her instincts, and to honor her needs. She realized that she didn't have to constantly strive for more or prove herself to anyone. She was enough, just as she was.

Embracing New Hobbies

With more space in her home and her mind, Emily also found room for new hobbies. She had always loved art, but she had never allowed herself the time to explore it. There were always more pressing things to do—work deadlines, social obligations, and endless errands. But now, with her simpler lifestyle, she had the freedom to pursue her passions.

She set up a small art station in a sunny corner of her apartment, complete with a sketchpad, watercolors, and a few brushes. At first, she felt a little silly—like a child playing with finger paints. But as she began to put brush to paper, she felt a wave of joy and creativity wash over her. She wasn't trying to create a masterpiece; she was just playing, experimenting, and expressing herself.

Emily found that painting was a form of meditation in itself. It allowed her to quiet her mind, focus on the present moment, and let go of perfectionism. She loved the way the colors flowed across the page, blending and shifting in unexpected ways. It reminded her that life, like art, was messy, unpredictable, and beautiful.

As she continued to explore her artistic side, Emily felt a sense of fulfillment that she hadn't felt in years. She realized that she didn't need a lot of things to be happy; she just needed the space and freedom to do what she loved. Painting became a regular part of her routine, a way to unwind, express herself, and connect with her creativity.

Volunteering and Giving Back

Another area that Emily wanted to explore was giving back to her community. She had always been passionate about social causes, but her busy life had left little time for volunteering. Now, with her simplified schedule and newfound clarity, she felt ready to make a difference.

She started by volunteering at a local community garden, helping to plant vegetables, weed beds, and harvest produce. It was hard work, but it was also incredibly rewarding. Emily loved being outside, getting her hands dirty, and working alongside other volunteers who shared her passion for sustainability and food justice.

Through her volunteer work, Emily also discovered a sense of connection and community that she hadn't realized she was missing. She met people from all walks of life, each with their own stories, struggles, and dreams. She learned about the challenges facing her community, from food insecurity to environmental degradation, and she felt inspired to be part of the solution.

Volunteering became a way for Emily to give back, but it also became a source of growth and learning. She discovered new skills, gained new perspectives, and developed a deeper appreciation for the interconnectedness of all things. It reminded her that minimalism wasn't just about decluttering her own life; it was about making space for others, contributing to something bigger than herself, and living in harmony with the world around her.

Deepening Relationships

As Emily continued to create space in her life, she also found herself reevaluating her relationships. Minimalism had taught her the importance of quality over quantity—of valuing depth over superficiality. She wanted her relationships to reflect that philosophy, to be meaningful, supportive, and authentic.

She began by reaching out to her closest friends, inviting them over for simple, intimate gatherings. Instead of going out to crowded bars or fancy restaurants, they would meet at her apartment, share a home-cooked meal, and spend hours talking, laughing, and connecting. These moments felt more genuine, more nourishing, and more aligned with her values.

Emily also made an effort to spend more time with her family. She realized that, in the past, she had often prioritized work, social events, and other commitments over her relationships with her parents and siblings. But now, with her focus on intentional living, she wanted to make them a priority.

She started visiting her parents more often, helping them with chores, cooking them dinner, and just spending time together. She called her siblings regularly, checking in on their lives, offering support, and sharing her own experiences. These simple acts of connection brought her closer to her family and deepened her sense of belonging and love.

At the same time, Emily also learned to let go of relationships that no longer served her. She recognized that some friendships were built on convenience rather than genuine connection, and that some people were more interested in what she could offer them than in who she was. It wasn't easy to say goodbye, but she knew it was necessary for her growth.

By creating space for the relationships that mattered and letting go of those that didn't, Emily found a new sense of clarity and fulfillment. She was surrounded by people who loved and supported her, who challenged her to grow, and who shared her values. And in those connections, she found a deeper sense of meaning and purpose.

Exploring New Possibilities

With each new step in her minimalist journey, Emily felt her world expanding. She was discovering new passions, forming deeper connections, and finding joy in simplicity. But she also knew that growth wasn't always linear. It wasn't just about adding new things to her life; it was about being open to change, to uncertainty, and to the unknown.

One day, while browsing a local bookstore, Emily came across a book on minimalism and travel. The author wrote about the freedom of living out of a backpack, exploring new cultures, and embracing the unknown. Emily felt a spark of excitement. She had always loved to travel, but her trips had often been rushed, filled with packed itineraries and countless souvenirs.

What if, instead of cramming as much as possible into each trip, she embraced a minimalist approach to travel? What if she focused on quality experiences rather than quantity, on connection rather than consumption?

Inspired, Emily decided to take a solo trip to a small village in the mountains, a place she had always wanted to visit but had never made time for. She packed lightly, bringing only the essentials, and set off with an open mind and an open heart.

The journey was transformative. Without the distractions of a busy itinerary or the burden of excess baggage, Emily found herself fully immersed in the experience. She hiked through lush forests, savored simple, delicious meals, and connected with locals who welcomed her with warmth and hospitality.

She also spent a lot of time alone, reflecting on her journey and her life. In the stillness of the mountains, she found a deep sense of peace and clarity. She realized that, just as in her minimalist lifestyle, travel was about intention, mindfulness, and being present in the moment.

When she returned home, Emily felt rejuvenated, inspired, and grateful. She had created space for growth, for exploration, and for new possibilities. And in that space, she had found a deeper sense of herself and her purpose.

Continuing the Journey

As Emily settled back into her routine, she knew that her journey was far from over. Minimalism wasn't a destination; it was a way of living, a continuous process of growth, learning, and discovery. She was excited to see where it would take her next.

She continued to meditate each morning, finding stillness and clarity in the quiet moments. She painted regularly, losing herself in the creative flow. She volunteered at the community garden, nurturing her connection to the earth and her community. She cherished her relationships, investing time and energy in the people who mattered most.

And she kept her heart open to new experiences, new challenges, and new opportunities for growth. She knew that life was unpredictable, that change was inevitable, and that growth required courage, curiosity, and an open mind.

But she also knew that, no matter what the future held, she had the tools, the mindset, and the space to face it with grace and intention. She had created a life that was simple, but full—a life that was grounded in her values, her passions, and her purpose.

And in that simplicity, she had found something truly extraordinary: the freedom to live authentically, to grow continuously, and to be fully, joyfully, and unapologetically herself.

# Chapter 21: The Minimalist Community

Emily had always thought of minimalism as a personal journey—a path she needed to walk alone, guided by her intuition and inspired by a few online blogs. But after nearly a year of living with less, she began to feel the need for something more, something communal. Her minimalist lifestyle had transformed her life, bringing clarity, purpose, and a surprising amount of joy. Yet, she longed for connection with others who understood the profound shift she had experienced.

One evening, as she scrolled through her email, Emily noticed an invitation to a local minimalist meet-up. It was a simple affair: a group of like-minded individuals gathering at a nearby park to share experiences and ideas. She hesitated for a moment, the introverted part of her unsure about meeting strangers. But the thought of connecting with others on the same path excited her. With a burst of determination, she replied to the email, confirming her attendance.

The day of the meet-up dawned clear and bright. Emily arrived at the park with a mix of nerves and anticipation. A small group of people had already gathered near a picnic table, their casual demeanor and relaxed smiles putting her at ease. As she approached, a tall man with a neatly trimmed beard and warm eyes extended his hand.

"Hey there! You must be Emily. I'm Marcus," he said with a welcoming smile.

"Nice to meet you, Marcus," Emily replied, shaking his hand. "I'm excited to be here. This is my first meet-up."

"Well, welcome to the minimalist community! We're glad to have you," Marcus said. "Feel free to grab a seat and make yourself comfortable."

Emily settled into a folding chair, taking in the diverse group around her. There was a young couple, both in their early thirties, with a toddler who was busily playing with a stick; a middle-aged woman with silver hair and a serene expression; a college student with a backpack slung over one shoulder; and a few others who looked equally intrigued and eager to share.

Marcus took a seat at the head of the table, clapping his hands together to get everyone's attention.

"All right, everyone, thank you for coming! It's great to see so many new faces today," he began. "Let's start with some introductions. Just tell us your name and a little about why you're interested in minimalism."

One by one, the attendees introduced themselves. When it was Emily's turn, she took a deep breath and spoke.

"I'm Emily. I've been on a minimalist journey for about a year now. It started with decluttering my closet and has since changed almost every aspect of my life. I'm here because I want to connect with others who are also embracing this lifestyle."

The group nodded in understanding, and Emily felt a wave of relief wash over her. These people got it. They understood the challenges, the triumphs, and the subtle, transformative shifts that came with choosing a simpler life.

As the introductions wrapped up, Marcus began to facilitate a discussion about the different aspects of minimalism. Emily listened intently, absorbing the variety of experiences and perspectives. Each person's journey was unique, shaped by their circumstances, desires, and values. Yet, there was a common thread of intentionality and purpose that wove their stories together.

Sharing Experiences

After about an hour of discussion, Marcus suggested they break into smaller groups to share more personal stories. Emily found herself paired with Clara, the silver-haired woman, and Jake, the college student. As they moved to a quieter corner of the park, Clara began to speak.

"I've been a minimalist for about five years now," Clara said, her voice calm and steady. "For me, it started as a way to cope with loss. My husband passed away suddenly, and I found myself drowning in the things we had accumulated over a lifetime. It was overwhelming. Letting go of those possessions helped me heal. It allowed me to focus on what truly mattered—the memories, not the objects."

Emily nodded, touched by Clara's story. "That's beautiful, Clara. I can relate in a way. For me, minimalism was a way to escape the chaos of my mind. My life was so cluttered, not just with things but with stress and anxiety. Simplifying my environment helped me find peace."

Jake, who had been listening quietly, chimed in. "For me, it's more about sustainability. I'm studying environmental science, and I've learned how harmful overconsumption is to our planet. I wanted to align my lifestyle with my values, so I started decluttering and reducing my waste. It's been a great experience so far, but it's challenging in a college setting where everyone's obsessed with the latest tech and trends."

Emily smiled, appreciating Jake's perspective. "It's amazing how minimalism can mean so many different things to different people. It's not just about having less but about having more of what truly matters."

The group continued to share their experiences, delving deeper into their motivations and challenges. Clara spoke about her journey toward mindfulness, Jake discussed his efforts to live more sustainably, and Emily shared her ongoing struggle to resist societal pressures to consume. As they talked, they discovered a shared desire for authenticity, simplicity, and connection.

Building Connections

As the afternoon wore on, Emily felt a sense of camaraderie growing among the group. She was surprised by how quickly she felt comfortable with these strangers, bonded by their shared values and experiences. It was a stark contrast to the superficial relationships she had once cultivated, based on convenience and mutual interest in material pursuits.

As the meet-up drew to a close, Marcus gathered everyone together again for a final reflection. "I want to thank you all for coming and for sharing so openly," he said. "It's not easy to break away from societal norms and embrace a different way of living. But when we come together like this, we realize we're not alone. We have a community."

Emily found herself nodding in agreement. She had come to the meet-up hoping to learn more about minimalism, but she had gained so much more—new friends, new perspectives, and a sense of belonging she hadn't realized she was missing.

As the group began to disperse, Marcus approached Emily with a smile. "Hey, we're planning to have a potluck next weekend, just a small gathering at my place. Would you like to join us?"

Emily hesitated for a moment, her introverted nature threatening to take over. But then she remembered how much she had enjoyed the day, how much she had gained from connecting with others on this journey.

"I'd love to," she replied, smiling. "Thank you for the invitation."

The Power of Community

Over the next few months, Emily became more involved in the minimalist community. She attended meet-ups, potlucks, and workshops, each gathering deepening her understanding of minimalism and her connection to those around her. She discovered a rich tapestry of stories, ideas, and experiences, each person's journey adding depth and color to her own.

At one potluck, Emily met Sarah, a single mother who had embraced minimalism as a way to simplify her life and focus on her children. Sarah spoke about the challenges of raising kids in a consumer-driven society and how she was teaching her children to value experiences over possessions.

"I used to feel guilty about not being able to buy my kids the latest toys or gadgets," Sarah admitted. "But then I realized that what they really needed was my time and attention. Now, instead of shopping for the latest toys, we spend our weekends hiking, baking, or just being together. It's brought us so much closer as a family."

Emily was inspired by Sarah's story. It was a powerful reminder that minimalism was not just about decluttering but about creating space for what truly mattered—love, connection, and presence.

At another gathering, Emily met Ravi, a tech entrepreneur who had decided to downsize his life after burning out from the relentless pace of his career. Ravi shared how he had sold his company, moved into a tiny house, and started a blog about minimalist living.

"I used to measure my success by how much money I made and how many things I owned," Ravi said. "But after my health started to decline, I realized that all of that was meaningless if I wasn't happy or healthy. Minimalism gave me a second chance. It allowed me to redefine success on my own terms."

Ravi's story resonated deeply with Emily. She had spent so much of her life chasing after external markers of success, never pausing to consider what truly made her happy. Minimalism had given her the freedom to explore those questions, to redefine her life according to her own values.

Organizing Events and Sharing the Message

Inspired by the stories she heard and the connections she made, Emily began to take a more active role in the community. She volunteered to help organize events, bringing her organizational skills and creative ideas to the table. She started a monthly book club focused on minimalist living and mindfulness, and she hosted a series of workshops on decluttering and sustainable living.

At one of these workshops, Emily decided to share her journey more publicly. Standing in front of a small audience, she spoke about her initial struggles with letting go, the emotional and psychological challenges she had faced, and the profound sense of freedom and clarity she had found through minimalism.

"It wasn't just about getting rid of stuff," she explained. "It was about letting go of the expectations and pressures that had been weighing me down for so long. It was about finding out who I really was, beneath all the layers of consumerism and societal norms."

The audience listened intently, nodding in agreement and understanding. Afterward, several people approached her, thanking her for sharing her story and offering their own experiences and insights.

One woman, a retiree named Helen, shared how minimalism had helped her navigate the transition from a busy career to a quieter life. "I had spent so many years defining myself by my job," Helen said. "When I retired, I felt lost. Minimalism helped me rediscover who I was outside of my career. It's given me a new lease on life."

A young man named Carlos spoke about his struggles with debt and how minimalism had helped him regain control of his finances. "I used to buy things to fill a void," he admitted. "But now, I focus on what truly brings me joy—spending time with friends, exploring nature, and pursuing my passions. Minimalism has been a game-changer for me."

As Emily listened to these stories, she realized just how powerful the minimalist philosophy could be. It wasn't just a trend or a lifestyle choice; it was a movement, a way of thinking that could transform lives and communities. She felt a deep sense of purpose and fulfillment, knowing that she was part of something much bigger than herself.

Spreading the Word

Emily's involvement in the minimalist community continued to grow. She started a blog to share her experiences and insights, hoping to inspire others to embrace a simpler, more intentional way of living. She wrote about the joys and challenges of minimalism, offering practical tips, personal reflections, and stories from the community.

To her surprise, the blog quickly gained a following. Readers from around the world reached out to her, sharing their own journeys and thanking her for the inspiration. Emily was humbled by the response and motivated to continue spreading the message of minimalism.

She collaborated with Marcus and other community members to organize larger events, including a minimalist fair that featured local artisans, sustainable products, and workshops on decluttering, mindfulness, and sustainable living. The event was a huge success, drawing hundreds of attendees and generating buzz in the local media.

As Emily stood at the entrance of the fair, watching people browse the booths and participate in the workshops, she felt a surge of pride and gratitude. This was the power of community, the power of coming together to share, learn, and grow. She realized that minimalism was not just about living with less but about living more—more connected, more intentional, and more aware.

The Ripple Effect

Over time, Emily noticed a ripple effect taking place. Friends and family who had once been skeptical of her minimalist lifestyle began to show interest. Her parents, who had initially been concerned about her decision to downsize, started asking questions and even attended a few meet-ups. Her colleagues at work, inspired by her calm demeanor and newfound clarity, asked for advice on decluttering and simplifying their own lives.

One day, her friend Lisa, who had always been a shopaholic, called her up. "Hey, Emily," Lisa began hesitantly, "I've been thinking a lot about what you've been doing with minimalism. I used to think it was just a phase, but now I see how happy and content you are. I want to try it too. Can you help me get started?"

Emily was thrilled. "Of course, Lisa! I'd love to help. We can start with a simple decluttering session and go from there."

As she hung up the phone, Emily couldn't help but smile. This was what it was all about—helping others find freedom and joy through simplicity. She realized that the minimalist community wasn't just a group of people; it was a movement, a revolution in how people lived, thought, and connected.

A Shared Vision for the Future

As the minimalist community continued to grow and evolve, Emily found herself reflecting on the journey that had brought her here. She thought about all the people she had met, the stories she had heard, and the impact they had made together. It was a journey of discovery, not just of herself but of the world around her.

One evening, as she sat with Marcus, Sarah, Ravi, and a few other community members around a bonfire, she shared her thoughts.

"You know, when I first started this journey, I thought minimalism was just about getting rid of stuff," she began, gazing into the flickering flames. "But now, I see it's so much more than that. It's about connection, community, and creating space for what truly matters. It's about living with intention and purpose, and helping others do the same."

The group nodded in agreement, their faces illuminated by the warm glow of the fire. Marcus raised his cup in a toast.

"To the minimalist community," he said. "To living simply, loving deeply, and creating a better world for ourselves and future generations."

"To the minimalist community," everyone echoed, clinking their cups together.

# Chapter 22: Minimalism in the Workplace

Emily arrived at her office building at 8:30 a.m., as usual, but today felt different. It was her first day back after a two-week vacation, a much-needed break that she had spent exploring the mountains with only a backpack and a camera. The trip had been a lesson in living with less, even more than she had anticipated. With each step up the trails, each breath of fresh air, Emily had felt herself shedding not only physical weight but mental clutter too.

Her minimalist journey had transformed many aspects of her life. At home, she had simplified her possessions and routine, finding a sense of calm she hadn't known in years. But as she stood in the lobby of her high-rise office building, surrounded by the familiar rush of professionals clutching their coffee cups and briefcases, she realized that her work life still felt as chaotic as ever.

As the elevator doors closed in front of her, she caught a glimpse of her reflection. Her expression was calm but determined. "Today," she thought, "things are going to change."

The Office Environment

Walking through the office, Emily noticed the usual sights and sounds: phones ringing, fingers tapping on keyboards, the hum of printers spitting out page after page. She passed by desks cluttered with stacks of papers, unopened mail, and personal trinkets. Many of her colleagues had photos, plants, or inspirational quotes plastered around their workspaces, creating a visual noise that seemed at odds with her newly adopted minimalist philosophy.

Emily's own desk wasn't much better. She had left in a hurry before her vacation, and it showed. A week's worth of reports and client presentations were scattered across the surface, and several half-used notebooks cluttered the drawer. She sighed, realizing how much her office environment reflected her old mindset — one of excess, accumulation, and disorganization.

Determined to change, she took a deep breath and started with a clean slate. She began by removing everything from her desk, placing it all in a box. It felt cathartic, like a fresh start. Then, she carefully selected only the essentials: her laptop, a notepad, a pen, and a small succulent plant that a friend had gifted her. The rest of the items were sorted into piles — one for recycling, another for storage, and a final pile for donations.

As she arranged her newly simplified desk, she felt a sense of relief. The clean, uncluttered space seemed to invite clarity and focus. She sat down, ready to tackle the day with a new sense of purpose.

A New Approach to Meetings

The first item on Emily's agenda was a team meeting with her department. As she entered the conference room, she noticed the usual setup: a long table covered with folders, laptops, and coffee cups. Her colleagues were engaged in small talk, waiting for the meeting to begin.

Emily decided to try something different. "Good morning, everyone," she began, standing at the head of the table. "Before we start, I'd like to introduce a new approach to our meetings. As some of you know, I've been exploring minimalism, and I think we can apply some of its principles here to make our meetings more efficient and productive."

A few raised eyebrows met her statement, but Emily continued. "For today's meeting, let's keep it simple. I've prepared a single-page agenda, and I'd like us to focus on just the three most important topics. We'll allocate ten minutes to each and keep our discussion concise. If there's anything that requires more time, we can schedule a follow-up."

The team members exchanged glances, but there were nods of agreement as well. Curious, they seemed willing to give it a try. Emily handed out the agenda, and they dove into the first topic.

To her surprise, the meeting flowed smoothly. By focusing on just a few key points, they were able to dive deeper into the issues that mattered most. There were fewer distractions, less meandering, and no time wasted on minor details. Within thirty minutes, they had covered all the topics, made decisions, and even outlined a plan of action for the coming week.

As the team members filed out of the room, several stopped to thank Emily for the efficient meeting. "That was great," one colleague said. "We should do this more often."

Emily smiled, feeling a sense of accomplishment. It was a small change, but it had made a big difference. She realized that minimalism wasn't just about decluttering her physical space; it was about simplifying processes and creating more focus in every aspect of her life, including work.

Streamlining Digital Clutter

Back at her desk, Emily turned her attention to her digital environment. Her email inbox was overflowing with unread messages, newsletters, and spam — a digital version of the clutter she had just cleared from her desk. She had always felt overwhelmed by the constant influx of emails, feeling like she could never quite keep up.

Determined to apply minimalist principles to her digital life as well, Emily decided to tackle her inbox with a new strategy. She set a goal to reach "inbox zero" by the end of the day.

First, she unsubscribed from all the newsletters and promotional emails she never read. It was a surprisingly liberating feeling, knowing she wouldn't be bombarded with unnecessary distractions anymore. Next, she created folders for different categories — clients, projects, administrative tasks — and began sorting her emails accordingly.

With a deep breath, Emily tackled the remaining emails one by one. She deleted those that were no longer relevant, responded to the ones that required quick replies, and flagged important ones for follow-up. By the end of the afternoon, her inbox was empty for the first time in years.

The sense of accomplishment was palpable. Emily felt a weight lift off her shoulders. With a streamlined digital environment, she found it easier to focus on her work without the constant distraction of a cluttered inbox.

Inspired by her success, she decided to extend her digital declutter to other areas. She organized her computer files, deleting duplicates and unnecessary documents. She cleaned up her bookmarks, keeping only the most frequently used links. And she even decided to limit her social media use, setting specific times to check her accounts rather than constantly scrolling throughout the day.

By the end of the week, Emily's digital world was as organized and simplified as her physical space. She felt more in control of her work, more focused, and more productive. The minimalist approach was proving to be a powerful tool for transforming not just her home life, but her professional life as well.

Redefining Productivity

As Emily continued to embrace minimalism in the workplace, she began to rethink her approach to productivity. In the past, she had equated being productive with being busy. She often felt pressured to fill her schedule with meetings, tasks, and projects, believing that a full calendar was a sign of success.

But as she delved deeper into minimalist principles, Emily began to question this mindset. She realized that true productivity wasn't about doing more; it was about doing less but with more focus and intention. It was about prioritizing the tasks that truly mattered and letting go of the rest.

With this new perspective, Emily decided to overhaul her approach to her to-do list. She started by identifying her top three priorities for the day — the tasks that would have the most significant impact on her work and align with her long-term goals. She focused on completing these tasks first, before moving on to anything else.

To her surprise, this simple shift made a huge difference. By focusing on her top priorities, Emily found that she was able to accomplish more in less time. She felt more energized and less stressed, no longer overwhelmed by an endless list of tasks. She also found that she had more time to think creatively and strategically, which led to better decision-making and more innovative ideas.

Emily's new approach didn't go unnoticed. Her colleagues began to see a change in her demeanor and her output. She was more focused in meetings, more decisive in her actions, and more present in her interactions. Her boss, impressed by her productivity and leadership, even asked her to share her strategies with the team.

Eager to spread the benefits of minimalism, Emily organized a workshop for her department. She introduced the concept of "essentialism" — focusing on what is truly essential and letting go of the rest. She shared her tips for prioritizing tasks, decluttering digital spaces, and simplifying workflows.

The response was overwhelmingly positive. Many of her colleagues were inspired to try out the minimalist approach themselves, eager to find a better balance between their work and personal lives. Emily felt a sense of fulfillment knowing that her journey was having a positive impact on those around her.

A Minimalist Office Culture

As Emily's influence grew, she began to envision a larger transformation. What if the entire office embraced minimalist principles? What if they could create a work environment that prioritized focus, clarity, and purpose over busyness and excess?

With the support of her boss, Emily set out to create a minimalist office culture. She started by redesigning the physical space, removing unnecessary furniture and creating open, clutter-free workstations. She introduced quiet zones for focused work and collaborative spaces for team meetings, encouraging a balance between individual productivity and teamwork.

Next, Emily worked with the leadership team to streamline workflows and reduce unnecessary bureaucracy. They implemented clear, concise communication strategies, reducing the number of meetings and emails and focusing on direct, meaningful interactions. They also encouraged flexible work arrangements, allowing employees to work remotely or adjust their schedules to better fit their needs.

The changes didn't happen overnight, but slowly, the office culture began to shift. Employees reported feeling more focused, more engaged, and more satisfied with their work. Productivity increased, but so did creativity and innovation. The office felt lighter, more energized, and more aligned with its goals.

Emily was thrilled to see the transformation taking place. She realized that minimalism wasn't just a personal philosophy; it was a powerful tool for creating a more efficient, effective, and fulfilling workplace. By simplifying processes, focusing on what truly mattered, and letting go of excess, they had created a work environment that supported both individual well-being and organizational success.

Challenges and Resistance

Of course, not everyone was on board with the changes. Some employees resisted the new approach, feeling uncomfortable with the shift away from traditional office norms. They missed the familiarity of their cluttered desks, the constant busyness, and the old ways of doing things.

Emily understood their concerns. Change was never easy, especially when it meant letting go of long-held habits and beliefs. She knew that minimalism could be challenging, requiring a shift in mindset and a willingness to embrace the unknown.

To support her colleagues through the transition, Emily organized regular feedback sessions, encouraging open dialogue and collaboration. She listened to their concerns, addressed their challenges, and provided guidance and support. She also shared her own experiences, being honest about the difficulties she had faced on her minimalist journey.

Slowly but surely, the resistance began to fade. As employees experienced the benefits of minimalism for themselves, they started to embrace the new approach. They found that a clutter-free environment made it easier to focus, that streamlined workflows reduced stress, and that prioritizing essential tasks led to greater satisfaction and success.

The Ripple Effect

As the minimalist culture took root, Emily noticed a ripple effect beyond the office walls. Her colleagues began to adopt minimalist principles in their personal lives as well, decluttering their homes, simplifying their routines, and finding more time for what truly mattered.

Emily herself felt more balanced and fulfilled than ever before. Her work was no longer a source of stress and overwhelm but a meaningful part of her life that aligned with her values and purpose. She had found a way to integrate minimalism into every aspect of her life, creating a harmonious balance between work and play, productivity and rest, doing and being.

Looking back on her journey, Emily felt a deep sense of gratitude. Minimalism had transformed her life in ways she had never imagined, bringing clarity, focus, and fulfillment to both her personal and professional worlds. She had learned that living with less didn't mean sacrificing success or ambition; it meant finding the freedom to pursue what truly mattered, with intention and purpose.

As she sat at her desk, now clean and uncluttered, Emily felt a renewed sense of energy and excitement. There were still challenges to face, still work to be done, but she was ready for whatever came next. With a minimalist mindset, she knew she had the tools to create a life of meaning, both inside and outside the office.

And as she looked around at her colleagues, now engaged in focused work, collaborative discussions, and creative problem-solving, Emily realized that the minimalist revolution was just beginning. Together, they were creating a new way of working, a new way of living, and a new way of being — one that prioritized clarity, purpose, and simplicity in every aspect of life.

# Chapter 23: A Sustainable Lifestyle

Emily stood in her kitchen, gazing at the small compost bin she had recently purchased. It was a simple item, but its significance loomed large. Over the past few months, she had become increasingly aware of the environmental impact of her choices. The more she embraced minimalism, the more she realized that true simplicity was not just about decluttering her home but also about making conscious decisions that reduced her footprint on the planet.

The journey to a sustainable lifestyle had begun with a single, seemingly trivial observation. Emily had noticed just how much waste she produced on a daily basis—food wrappers, plastic bottles, disposable coffee cups. It seemed contradictory to her minimalist values to create so much waste. After all, minimalism was about living with less and focusing on what truly mattered. How could she claim to live simply when her lifestyle contributed to environmental degradation?

The shift had started with a documentary she watched one evening about plastic pollution. The images of oceans choked with plastic debris, marine animals struggling amidst discarded waste, and communities suffering the effects of pollution hit her hard. She couldn't stop thinking about it. The next day, she found herself in a conversation with Aaron about the documentary.

"I've been thinking a lot about sustainability," she said, stirring her tea thoughtfully. "It feels like a natural extension of minimalism, don't you think? Living with less, being more intentional—it should apply to the environment too."

Aaron nodded. "Absolutely. Minimalism and sustainability go hand in hand. It's about being mindful of our choices, not just for ourselves but for the planet too."

Emily had always admired Aaron's thoughtful approach to minimalism. He wasn't just about reducing possessions; he was about enhancing life quality through mindful decisions. His words resonated deeply with her, reinforcing her commitment to expand her minimalist journey into the realm of sustainability.

Shifting Mindsets: From Convenience to Consciousness

Emily's first step towards sustainability was confronting her reliance on single-use plastics. She started carrying a reusable water bottle and coffee cup, refusing plastic bags at the grocery store, and opting for loose produce instead of pre-packaged items. These small changes made her more aware of the pervasive presence of plastic in her life and the convenience-driven choices she had been making without thinking.

The more she learned, the more she realized that her previous habits were not just wasteful but also contrary to her new values. Each time she chose reusable over disposable, she felt a small sense of victory. It wasn't always easy; habits were hard to break, and there were moments of frustration. Like the day she forgot her reusable bag and had to carry groceries in her arms, or when she realized how much she missed the convenience of pre-packaged snacks. But every challenge reinforced her determination to live more sustainably.

Emily began researching sustainable practices, immersing herself in articles, documentaries, and books about the environment. She learned about the carbon footprint of different foods, the benefits of buying local, and the impact of fast fashion on the planet. The more she learned, the more she wanted to change.

The Transformation of Home and Habits

One of Emily's biggest challenges was rethinking her approach to food. She had always loved cooking, but her habits were far from sustainable. Pre-packaged meals, imported produce, and an overreliance on meat and dairy were staples in her diet. Determined to make a change, Emily began experimenting with plant-based recipes, incorporating more local and seasonal produce into her meals.

She discovered the joy of visiting farmers' markets, where she could buy fresh, locally grown produce directly from the people who grew it. It wasn't just about reducing her carbon footprint; it was about supporting her community and connecting with her food in a more meaningful way. The vibrant colors and flavors of the seasonal produce were a revelation, and she found herself getting excited about cooking in a way she hadn't before.

One weekend, Emily decided to take her commitment to sustainability a step further by starting a small vegetable garden on her apartment balcony. She had never considered herself much of a gardener, but the idea of growing her own food, even just a little, appealed to her newfound desire for self-sufficiency and sustainability.

She began with a few pots of herbs—basil, mint, and rosemary—along with some cherry tomatoes and lettuce. The initial setup was simple, but it was a start. Aaron, who had been gardening for years, offered her advice and encouragement. "Start small," he had told her. "Gardening is about patience and learning. It's not just about the harvest; it's about the process."

Over the following weeks, Emily watched with fascination as her plants began to grow. She watered them diligently, carefully monitored their progress, and even started composting her kitchen scraps to create nutrient-rich soil. The process of nurturing her plants became a meditative practice, a way to connect with nature in the midst of her urban life.

Fashioning a Sustainable Wardrobe

Emily's commitment to sustainability extended beyond her kitchen and balcony. Her wardrobe, once a source of pride and identity, had undergone a significant transformation since she began her minimalist journey. The initial decluttering had left her with only the clothes she loved and actually wore, but now she wanted her wardrobe to reflect her values as well.

She learned about the devastating impact of fast fashion on the environment and the people who made the clothes. The staggering waste, the pollution, and the exploitative labor practices were enough to make her rethink her relationship with fashion entirely. She realized that just as she had been a mindless consumer of goods, she had also been a mindless consumer of fashion.

Instead of buying new clothes, Emily began exploring second-hand stores and vintage shops. She was pleasantly surprised by the unique pieces she found, items with a history and a story. She discovered the joy of wearing clothes that were well-made and built to last, rather than cheap, disposable fashion. It was a radical shift from her previous mindset, but it felt right.

She also started researching ethical and sustainable clothing brands. When she did buy something new, she made sure it was from a company that prioritized environmental responsibility and fair labor practices. It wasn't always easy—sustainable fashion could be more expensive, and the choices were limited—but Emily found satisfaction in knowing that her purchases aligned with her values.

Navigating the Challenges of Change

As Emily's commitment to sustainability deepened, she faced new challenges and resistance. Not everyone around her understood or appreciated her choices. Some friends teased her about her "hippie" lifestyle, while others rolled their eyes at her efforts to reduce waste and buy organic.

At family gatherings, she often found herself at odds with relatives who didn't see the point in making sustainable choices. During one such gathering, Emily's aunt, a woman who prided herself on her practicality, scoffed at her plant-based diet. "Oh, come on, Emily," she said. "A little meat never hurt anyone. You're taking this whole thing too far."

Emily took a deep breath, reminding herself that change was often met with resistance. "I understand where you're coming from, Aunt Karen," she replied calmly. "But for me, it's about more than just diet. It's about making choices that are better for the planet and for my health. I'm not trying to preach; I'm just trying to live in a way that feels right for me."

Despite the pushback, Emily found strength in her community. She joined local environmental groups and attended workshops on sustainable living. She met people who shared her values and passions, people who understood the importance of collective action. Together, they organized clean-ups, advocated for plastic bans, and promoted sustainable practices in their community.

The Intersection of Minimalism and Sustainability

Emily's journey towards sustainability had not been without its struggles, but it had also been incredibly rewarding. She realized that minimalism and sustainability were not just compatible; they were deeply interconnected. Both philosophies emphasized intentionality, mindfulness, and a focus on what truly mattered.

As she decluttered her life, Emily found that she naturally gravitated towards more sustainable choices. She no longer felt the need to buy things she didn't need or want, and she became more mindful of the impact of her actions on the world around her. It wasn't just about reducing waste; it was about living with a sense of purpose and responsibility.

One day, as she sat in her small but thriving balcony garden, Emily reflected on how far she had come. She had started her minimalist journey as a way to simplify her life and reduce stress, but it had become so much more than that. It had become a way to live in harmony with her values, to be more connected to her community, and to make a positive impact on the world.

Emily knew she wasn't perfect. There were still areas where she could improve, still choices that weren't as sustainable as they could be. But she also knew that sustainability, like minimalism, was a journey, not a destination. It was about making progress, not perfection, about being mindful and intentional, not rigid or dogmatic.

She realized that living sustainably wasn't about sacrificing joy or convenience; it was about finding joy in the simple things, in the things that truly mattered. It was about cherishing the earth and all its beauty, about being a steward of the planet for future generations.

A Ripple Effect of Change

Emily's commitment to sustainability began to inspire those around her. Her friends, who had once teased her for her "extreme" lifestyle, started to ask questions and make small changes of their own. One of her closest friends, Lisa, decided to try a month of plastic-free living after seeing Emily's dedication.

At first, Lisa was skeptical. "I don't know how you do it, Emily," she confessed. "It seems so hard to avoid plastic. It's everywhere!"

Emily smiled, remembering her own struggles when she first started. "It's definitely challenging at first," she admitted. "But it's also really rewarding. You start to notice how much plastic we use without thinking and how many alternatives there are once you start looking."

Lisa took up the challenge, and to her surprise, she found it was easier than she thought. She discovered reusable bags and produce pouches, started making her own cleaning products, and found a local zero-waste store where she could buy pantry staples in bulk. By the end of the month, she was hooked.

"It's amazing," Lisa told Emily. "I never realized how much waste I was creating. Now I'm more conscious of everything I buy and use. I feel like I'm making a difference, even if it's just a small one."

Emily was thrilled to see her friend's transformation. She realized that change often started with one person and could spread like ripples in a pond. Her own journey had been inspired by others, and now she was inspiring those around her. It was a reminder that every action, no matter how small, had the potential to create positive change.

Living with Purpose and Joy

As Emily's commitment to sustainability deepened, so did her sense of fulfillment and joy. She found that living in alignment with her values brought a sense of peace and contentment she had never known before. She no longer felt the need to keep up with the latest trends or buy things she didn't need. Instead, she found joy in the simple pleasures of life—a home-cooked meal, a walk in nature, a quiet moment in her garden.

She began to see her minimalist and sustainable lifestyle not as a sacrifice but as a gift. It was a gift to herself, a way to live more mindfully and meaningfully. It was a gift to the planet, a way to reduce her impact and protect the earth for future generations. And it was a gift to her community, a way to inspire others to live more consciously and sustainably.

One evening, Emily hosted a small dinner party for her friends, serving a meal made entirely from local, organic ingredients. As they sat around the table, laughing and sharing stories, she looked around at the faces of the people she loved. She realized that this was what it was all about—connecting with others, living with purpose, and finding joy in the simple things.

As the evening drew to a close, Aaron raised his glass. "To Emily," he said, smiling. "For inspiring us all to live more mindfully and sustainably."

Emily blushed, feeling a surge of gratitude and humility. "Thank you," she said, her voice filled with emotion. "But it's not just me. We're all on this journey together, and every step we take, no matter how small, makes a difference."

The room erupted in cheers, and Emily felt a deep sense of fulfillment. She knew that the journey towards sustainability was ongoing, that there would always be more to learn and more to do. But she also knew that she was on the right path, a path that brought her closer to her true self and to the world around her.

Embracing the Future

As Emily continued to explore sustainable living, she realized that her journey was far from over. There were still challenges to face and lessons to learn. But she was excited for the future, eager to discover new ways to live more sustainably and to inspire others to do the same.

She knew that sustainability wasn't just about individual actions; it was about systemic change. It was about advocating for policies and practices that protected the environment and promoted social justice. It was about building a world where everyone had access to clean air, water, and food, where communities could thrive without sacrificing the planet.

Emily decided to get more involved in local activism, joining a group that advocated for renewable energy and sustainable development. She attended rallies, spoke at community meetings, and even wrote a few op-eds for the local paper. She found that her passion for sustainability extended beyond her personal choices; it was about creating a better world for everyone.

She also continued to educate herself, reading books, attending workshops, and learning from others who were further along the path. She realized that sustainability was a journey of continuous learning and growth, a journey that required humility, curiosity, and a willingness to change.

As she looked ahead, Emily felt a deep sense of hope. She knew that the challenges were great, but she also knew that there was a growing movement of people who were committed to making a difference. She was proud to be a part of that movement, proud to live a life that reflected her values and made a positive impact on the world.

She knew that she couldn't change the world on her own, but she also knew that every action, no matter how small, mattered. Every time she chose reusable over disposable, every time she cooked a plant-based meal, every time she spoke out for environmental justice, she was contributing to a better future.

And that, she realized, was what sustainability was all about—not just living with less, but living with more. More intention, more purpose, more joy. It was about embracing the present and the future, about finding balance and harmony in a world that was often chaotic and uncertain.

And with that, she smiled, knowing that she was exactly where she was meant to be.

# Chapter 24: Reconnecting with Purpose

Emily awoke to the soft glow of the morning sun filtering through the sheer curtains of her minimalist apartment. The walls, painted in a calming shade of sage green, were adorned with only a few cherished pieces of art. Her bed, a simple wooden frame with a white duvet, was neatly made. The space felt open and airy, a stark contrast to the cluttered environment she once inhabited. She took a deep breath, feeling a sense of peace she had never experienced before her minimalist journey.

Today was significant for Emily, though not because of any planned events or obligations. It was a day she had set aside for herself—a day to pause, reflect, and reconnect with her deeper purpose. Over the past year, Emily had transformed her life in ways she never thought possible. She had decluttered her home, streamlined her routines, cultivated meaningful relationships, and even inspired others to explore the minimalist lifestyle. Yet, amidst all these changes, she realized there was still an underlying question she hadn't fully addressed: What was her true purpose?

Emily made her way to the small kitchen and prepared a simple breakfast of oatmeal topped with fresh berries and honey. She savored each bite, practicing the mindful eating habits she had developed. After finishing her meal, she brewed a cup of herbal tea and carried it to her favorite spot—the cozy corner by the window, where a soft armchair awaited her. She sat down, cradling the warm cup in her hands, and gazed out at the city below.

The view from her apartment, located on the outskirts of the bustling metropolis, offered a mix of urban life and nature. Tall buildings stretched toward the sky, while in the distance, a patch of green—a small park—provided a soothing contrast. Emily watched as the early morning joggers made their rounds and children played on the swings. The sight brought a smile to her face, reminding her of the simple joys in life.

As she sipped her tea, Emily opened her journal—a practice she had grown to cherish. The pages were filled with thoughts, reflections, and sketches, chronicling her journey toward minimalism and the lessons she had learned along the way. Today, however, she intended to go deeper. She wanted to explore the essence of her being, to uncover what truly drove her and gave her life meaning.

She began by writing a question at the top of a fresh page: "What is my purpose?" The words stared back at her, challenging her to dig beneath the surface of her day-to-day existence.

Emily closed her eyes and took a few deep breaths, centering herself. She recalled a meditation exercise Aaron had taught her, one that helped her focus on her inner voice. As she breathed in, she visualized inhaling clarity and understanding; as she breathed out, she released doubt and confusion.

She let her thoughts flow freely, jotting down whatever came to mind:

Connection: She had always valued her relationships with others. The support and love she shared with friends, family, and even strangers had been a constant source of joy and fulfillment.

Creativity: Emily realized that creativity had played a vital role in her life, from her love of writing and art to her innovative problem-solving at work. Creating brought her a sense of accomplishment and satisfaction.

Growth: The past year had taught her the importance of growth, both personal and professional. She thrived on learning new things, challenging herself, and evolving into a better version of herself.

Contribution: Perhaps most importantly, Emily felt a deep desire to make a positive impact on the world. Whether through volunteering, mentoring, or advocating for a cause, she found purpose in contributing to the greater good.

As she reviewed her notes, Emily saw a pattern emerging. Her purpose seemed to revolve around connecting with others, expressing her creativity, growing as an individual, and contributing to something larger than herself. But how could she weave these elements together into a cohesive vision for her life?

Suddenly, Emily's phone buzzed, interrupting her thoughts. She glanced at the screen and saw a message from Aaron: "Hey, Emily! Just checking in. How's your day of reflection going? Need any company?"

Emily smiled, appreciating the gesture. Aaron had been a constant source of support and wisdom throughout her journey, guiding her through the highs and lows of minimalism. She quickly typed a reply: "Thanks, Aaron. It's going well so far. Just digging deep into some big questions. Would love to chat later."

As she set her phone aside, Emily's thoughts returned to her journal. She realized that while the notes she had written were important, they were still somewhat abstract. She needed to ground them in something tangible, something actionable.

Emily decided to take a walk in the park. Nature had a way of clearing her mind and helping her see things more clearly. She grabbed her coat and headed out, breathing in the crisp autumn air as she made her way down the street. The park, with its golden leaves and serene atmosphere, was exactly what she needed.

She strolled along the winding paths, observing the beauty around her. The vibrant colors of the trees, the gentle rustling of the leaves, and the distant laughter of children all contributed to a sense of tranquility.

As she walked, Emily reflected on the four themes she had identified: connection, creativity, growth, and contribution.

She paused by a small pond and sat on a bench, watching the ducks glide across the water. It occurred to her that these elements weren't separate or independent; they were interconnected, like threads woven into a tapestry. Her purpose wasn't about choosing one over the other but about finding a way to integrate them into a cohesive whole.

Emily closed her eyes and took a deep breath, allowing herself to enter a meditative state. She imagined herself standing at a crossroads, with four paths stretching out before her, each representing one of the themes she had identified. She visualized herself walking down each path, exploring what it might look like to fully embrace that aspect of her purpose.

First, she imagined the path of connection. She saw herself surrounded by loved ones, building meaningful relationships based on trust, empathy, and support. She envisioned herself listening deeply, offering a shoulder to lean on, and creating a sense of community wherever she went. This path felt warm and comforting, like a hug from a close friend.

Next, she stepped onto the path of creativity. Here, she saw herself immersed in the act of creation, whether writing, painting, or coming up with innovative solutions to challenges. She felt the thrill of bringing something new into the world, of expressing herself authentically and unapologetically. This path was vibrant and dynamic, filled with color and movement.

Then, she walked down the path of growth. On this path, she saw herself constantly learning, evolving, and pushing her boundaries. She envisioned herself taking on new challenges, embracing discomfort, and celebrating her progress along the way. This path was steep and winding, but it offered breathtaking views and a sense of accomplishment.

Finally, she explored the path of contribution. Here, she saw herself giving back to others, using her skills and resources to make a positive impact. She imagined herself mentoring younger colleagues, volunteering at local charities, and advocating for causes she believed in. This path was wide and open, with many forks and intersections, symbolizing the endless possibilities for making a difference.

As Emily stood at the crossroads, she realized that she didn't have to choose just one path. Instead, she could create her own, a unique blend of all four, guided by her values and passions. Her purpose wasn't a destination but a journey—one that would evolve and change as she grew and learned.

With this newfound clarity, Emily opened her eyes and looked around. The park seemed even more beautiful than before, its colors more vibrant, its sounds more harmonious. She felt a deep sense of gratitude for the journey she had undertaken and for the lessons she had learned along the way.

As she made her way back home, Emily felt lighter, as if a weight had been lifted from her shoulders. She knew that her purpose wasn't something to be found or discovered but something to be created, nurtured, and lived every day.

Back in her apartment, Emily sat down at her desk and opened her journal once more. She began to write, not a list of goals or objectives but a personal manifesto—a statement of intent that captured the essence of her purpose.

"I am here to connect with others, to build meaningful relationships based on empathy, trust, and support. I am here to create, to express myself authentically and to bring new ideas into the world. I am here to grow, to learn, and to push my boundaries, embracing discomfort as a catalyst for transformation. I am here to contribute, to use my skills and resources to make a positive impact on the world around me.

"My purpose is not a destination but a journey, one that is guided by my values and fueled by my passions. I am committed to living each day with intention, to being present in every moment, and to honoring the unique path I am creating for myself."

As she finished writing, Emily felt a sense of fulfillment wash over her. She knew that her purpose would continue to evolve, but for now, she felt aligned with her true self. She closed her journal and placed it on her desk, feeling a renewed sense of direction and motivation.

Her phone buzzed again, and this time it was a call from Aaron. She answered with a smile, eager to share her insights and hear his thoughts.

"Hey, Emily! How's your day of reflection going?" Aaron's voice was warm and cheerful, as always.

"It's been amazing," Emily replied. "I feel like I've finally reconnected with my purpose. It's not just one thing; it's a combination of connection, creativity, growth, and contribution. I've realized that I don't have to choose just one path—I can create my own, blending all the things that matter to me."

"That's incredible, Emily," Aaron said, his voice filled with pride. "It sounds like you've really found a deeper understanding of what drives you. And the best part is, your purpose will continue to evolve as you do. It's a lifelong journey."

"Exactly," Emily agreed. "I'm excited to see where it takes me. I feel like I'm just getting started."

They talked for a while longer, sharing stories and ideas about how to live with intention and purpose. Emily felt a deep sense of gratitude for Aaron's friendship and support. He had been there for her every step of the way, guiding her through the challenges and celebrating her successes.

After they hung up, Emily stood by the window, gazing out at the city once more. The sun was setting, casting a warm golden light over the landscape. She felt a sense of peace and contentment, knowing that she was on the right path—one that was uniquely hers.

As the day drew to a close, Emily reflected on all the ways her life had changed since she embraced minimalism. She had let go of the excess, simplified her surroundings, and redefined her priorities. But more importantly, she had reconnected with her purpose, finding meaning and fulfillment in the journey.

She knew that challenges would arise and that there would be moments of doubt and uncertainty. But she also knew that she had the tools and the mindset to navigate them with grace and resilience. Her purpose was her compass, guiding her toward a life of simplicity, intention, and joy.

With a smile, Emily turned away from the window and began to prepare dinner, feeling a renewed sense of energy and enthusiasm. She knew that the journey ahead would be full of surprises and adventures, but she was ready to embrace it all with an open heart and an open mind.

As she sat down to eat, she whispered a silent thank you to herself, to Aaron, and to the universe for all the gifts she had received. She knew that she was exactly where she needed to be, living a life that was rich in meaning and aligned with her true purpose.

And for that, she was deeply, profoundly grateful.

# Chapter 25: The Ripple Effect

Emily sat on the edge of her favorite armchair, its faded blue fabric a testament to years of use and comfort. She cradled a cup of herbal tea, savoring its warmth as she gazed out of her window. The first rays of dawn were breaking over the horizon, casting a soft, golden light over the city. It was in these quiet moments, before the world fully awoke, that Emily felt most connected to herself and the path she had chosen.

It had been three years since she embarked on her minimalist journey, and in that time, her life had transformed in ways she never could have imagined. She had started with decluttering her wardrobe, then her home, and eventually her mind. Each step had been a revelation, peeling back layers of excess to reveal a clearer, more purposeful life underneath.

But perhaps the most surprising part of her journey was the effect it had on those around her. Emily hadn't set out to change anyone but herself, yet her transformation had inspired a ripple effect that extended far beyond her small apartment.

The Shift at Work

The first signs of this ripple effect began at work. Emily worked as a project manager for a mid-sized tech company, where long hours and high stress were the norms. In the past, she had thrown herself into her work, equating busyness with productivity and success. But as she embraced minimalism, she started to question this mindset.

Instead of filling her calendar with endless meetings and tasks, Emily began to prioritize her work based on its importance and alignment with her core values. She introduced the concept of "essentialism" to her team, encouraging them to focus on what truly mattered rather than getting bogged down in busywork.

At first, there was resistance. Her colleagues were skeptical, unable to see how doing less could lead to more effective results. But over time, they began to notice the changes in Emily. She was calmer, more focused, and less prone to burnout. She was still achieving her goals, but now she did so with a sense of ease that was both enviable and contagious.

Emily's approach started to catch on. Her team members began adopting her methods, cutting out unnecessary tasks and meetings, and focusing on high-impact work. They started to see improvements not just in their productivity, but also in their overall job satisfaction. As the team flourished, the company took notice.

Emily was invited to lead a workshop on minimalist principles and how they could be applied to project management. It was a daunting task—public speaking had never been her strong suit—but she saw it as an opportunity to share the benefits of minimalism on a larger scale.

The workshop was a resounding success. Employees from different departments expressed interest in applying these principles to their own work, and soon, the company was implementing a more minimalist approach across the board. Meetings were shorter and more focused, emails were concise, and the emphasis was placed on deep work rather than multitasking.

The company's culture began to shift. There was a noticeable decrease in stress and an increase in employee engagement. People had more time for creative thinking and innovation, and the quality of their work improved. Emily realized that her personal journey toward minimalism had sparked a change within her professional environment, and she felt a deep sense of fulfillment knowing she had made a positive impact.

Friends and Family

The ripple effect extended beyond the workplace and into Emily's personal life. Her friends had watched her transformation with a mix of curiosity and skepticism. They couldn't understand why she would give up so many of her possessions or why she preferred quiet evenings at home over a night out. But as they saw the positive changes in her demeanor and outlook, they began to ask questions.

One friend, Sarah, had been particularly resistant. A self-proclaimed shopaholic, Sarah loved fashion and the thrill of a good sale. Her closet was overflowing with clothes, many still with tags attached, and she often joked about her "retail therapy" sessions. When Emily first started talking about minimalism, Sarah brushed it off as just another trend.

But over time, Sarah noticed something she couldn't ignore: Emily seemed genuinely happier. She was less stressed, more present, and more content. It wasn't just the lack of clutter in her home; it was the lightness in her spirit that intrigued Sarah.

One afternoon, over coffee, Sarah confided in Emily. "I've been feeling overwhelmed lately," she admitted, her voice tinged with frustration. "It's like I have all this stuff, but I still feel empty. How did you do it, Em? How did you let go of everything?"

Emily smiled, sensing an opening. "It wasn't easy," she said gently. "But I started by asking myself what really matters to me. It wasn't about getting rid of things for the sake of it. It was about creating space for what's truly important."

Sarah listened intently as Emily shared her journey, the ups and downs, the challenges and triumphs. By the end of their conversation, Sarah was intrigued enough to give it a try. She started small, with her overflowing closet. Emily helped her sort through her clothes, encouraging her to keep only what she loved and actually wore.

The process was emotional. Sarah struggled with letting go of items she had bought impulsively or kept out of guilt. But as the piles of clothes to donate grew, so did her sense of relief. She realized that by holding on to all this excess, she was holding herself back.

Inspired by her first taste of minimalism, Sarah decided to extend her decluttering to other areas of her life. She cleared out her kitchen, organized her office, and even took a break from social media to focus on more meaningful connections. Over time, she too began to experience the benefits of a simpler, more intentional life.

Other friends followed suit. Some were drawn to the idea of decluttering their homes, while others were interested in adopting a more mindful approach to their daily routines. Emily became a resource, offering guidance and support to those looking to simplify their lives. She never pushed or preached; she simply shared her experiences and let others find their own path.

Her family was a different story. Her parents, particularly her mother, had been baffled by her decision to downsize her living space and embrace a minimalist lifestyle. They worried that she was making her life harder than it needed to be, depriving herself of comforts and conveniences.

But over time, even they began to see the benefits. When they visited Emily's new apartment, they were struck by how calm and serene it felt. The space was small but cozy, filled only with items that brought her joy or served a purpose. There was no clutter, no excess, just a sense of peace that was palpable.

Emily's mother, a collector by nature, was initially resistant to the idea of minimalism. She had spent years accumulating things—antiques, souvenirs, trinkets—that filled every corner of her home. But after seeing the change in Emily, she began to question her own attachment to her possessions.

One weekend, Emily offered to help her mother declutter her attic, a space that had become a catch-all for years of accumulated items. They spent hours sorting through boxes, laughing over old memories and reminiscing about family vacations. Her mother was reluctant at first, but as they worked together, she began to see the value in letting go.

By the end of the weekend, the attic was noticeably emptier, but her mother's heart felt lighter. She realized that her memories weren't tied to the things she owned but to the experiences and people that had shaped her life. Inspired by Emily's example, she continued to declutter her home, finding joy in creating a space that was both beautiful and functional.

Community Impact

As Emily's minimalist journey continued, the ripple effect began to extend even further, reaching her local community. She had become more involved in the minimalist community, organizing events and workshops to share her knowledge and experiences. She had started a blog, documenting her journey and offering tips for those interested in simplifying their lives.

Her blog quickly gained a following, resonating with people who were tired of the consumerist culture and looking for a more meaningful way to live. Emily received emails from readers all over the world, thanking her for inspiring them to make changes in their own lives. Some had started decluttering their homes, while others had embraced mindful living or sustainable practices.

Encouraged by the response, Emily decided to take her message offline and into her local community. She organized a "Declutter Day," inviting neighbors to bring items they no longer needed to a local park for a community-wide swap and donation event. The idea was simple: give what you don't need, take what you do, and donate the rest to charity.

The event was a huge success. People from all walks of life came together, sharing stories and exchanging items. There was a sense of camaraderie and support, a recognition that they were all on a journey toward a simpler, more intentional life.

The event sparked a series of community initiatives. Inspired by the Declutter Day, a group of residents started a monthly clothing swap, where people could exchange clothes they no longer wore for new-to-them items. Another group organized a "Fix-It Fair," where volunteers helped repair broken items to give them a second life rather than throwing them away.

Emily also collaborated with a local environmental group to promote sustainable living. They hosted workshops on composting, gardening, and reducing waste, encouraging residents to adopt eco-friendly practices in their daily lives. The response was overwhelmingly positive, and the community began to embrace a more sustainable lifestyle.

The ripple effect continued to spread. Schools started incorporating lessons on minimalism and sustainability into their curriculums, teaching students the value of living with less and caring for the environment. Local businesses began to adopt more sustainable practices, reducing waste and offering products that aligned with minimalist values.

Emily was amazed at how her personal journey had sparked such a widespread movement. She had never set out to change the world; she had simply wanted to change her own life. But in doing so, she had inspired others to do the same, creating a ripple effect that extended far beyond her own circle.

Global Influence

The impact of Emily's journey didn't stop at her community. Thanks to the reach of her blog and social media, her message of minimalism began to spread globally. People from all corners of the world were drawn to the simplicity and intentionality she espoused, and many were inspired to embark on their own minimalist journeys.

Emily was invited to speak at conferences and events around the world, sharing her story and the principles of minimalism with diverse audiences. She traveled to different countries, meeting people from all walks of life who were interested in simplifying their lives and finding more meaning in less.

In Japan, she met a young couple who had adopted a minimalist lifestyle after being inspired by her blog. They had downsized from a large house to a small apartment, finding joy in living with only the essentials. They shared how minimalism had helped them focus on their relationship and their passions, rather than being consumed by material possessions.

In Denmark, Emily spoke at a sustainability conference, where she met a group of activists who were using minimalism as a tool for environmental change. They believed that by reducing consumption and living more intentionally, people could significantly reduce their carbon footprint and contribute to a healthier planet.

In India, she visited a community that had embraced minimalism as a way of life for generations. They shared stories of how they had always lived simply, valuing experiences and relationships over possessions. Emily was struck by the realization that minimalism wasn't a new concept—it was a return to a way of life that many cultures had practiced for centuries.

These experiences broadened Emily's perspective, deepening her understanding of minimalism as a global movement. She saw that, at its core, minimalism was about more than just decluttering or simplifying. It was about reconnecting with what truly mattered, finding joy in the simple things, and living in harmony with oneself and the world.

Reflections and Gratitude

As Emily reflected on the ripple effect of her journey, she felt a deep sense of gratitude. She was grateful for the people she had met, the lessons she had learned, and the positive impact she had been able to make. She realized that her journey wasn't just about her own personal growth; it was about contributing to a larger movement toward a more mindful, intentional, and sustainable way of life.

She thought about Aaron, her mentor and friend, who had first introduced her to the minimalist philosophy. He had always believed in the power of one person to make a difference, and now she understood what he meant. By changing herself, she had changed her world, and in doing so, had inspired others to do the same.

Emily knew that her journey wasn't over. Minimalism was not a destination but a continuous process of learning, growing, and evolving. She was excited to see where the path would lead her next and how she could continue to make a positive impact.

As the sun rose higher in the sky, filling her apartment with light, Emily felt a sense of peace and fulfillment. She had found her purpose, not in the pursuit of more but in the joy of less. And in sharing that joy with others, she had created a ripple effect that would continue to spread, touching lives and inspiring change for years to come.

Emily took a sip of her tea, savoring the moment.

## Chapter 26: The Minimalist Revolution

The morning light filtered through Emily's minimalist apartment, casting soft beams across the uncluttered floor. She stood by the window, gazing out at the bustling city below, her reflection merging with the skyline. The journey that had begun with a chaotic wardrobe full of unworn clothes and an overwhelming sense of dissatisfaction had led her here, to this moment of quiet contemplation and profound clarity.

Emily's life had changed in ways she could never have imagined. The once cluttered apartment was now a serene haven of simplicity, a testament to her transformation. Each piece of furniture had a purpose, each item a story. Her space, once a symbol of consumer culture, now embodied the essence of minimalism. It was a life lived with intention, grounded in purpose and filled with contentment.

She sipped her tea slowly, savoring the warmth that spread through her hands. The ritual of a quiet morning had become one of her greatest joys, a moment of mindfulness that anchored her days. As she glanced around her apartment, she felt a surge of gratitude for everything she had gained by letting go.

Emily's minimalist journey had been about far more than just decluttering her physical space. It had been a profound reimagining of her values and priorities. She had stripped away the excess to reveal the essence of what truly mattered. In doing so, she had discovered a new way of living—one that resonated deeply with her soul and aligned with her innermost values.

Reconnecting with Purpose

Over the past few months, Emily had dedicated herself to helping others discover the power of minimalism. She had become a prominent voice in the minimalist community, organizing workshops and meetups, sharing her story, and encouraging others to embark on their journeys of self-discovery. She found fulfillment in guiding others, helping them to see beyond the allure of materialism and embrace a life of simplicity and purpose.

One of her greatest joys had been witnessing the ripple effect of her transformation. Friends, family, and even colleagues had been inspired by her journey, each finding their path toward a more intentional life. It was a powerful reminder of how change could start with one person and spread to many, like a single pebble creating ripples in a pond.

Aaron, her mentor, and friend had been a constant source of support and wisdom. He had taught her that minimalism was not about deprivation but about abundance—the abundance of time, space, and freedom that came from letting go of what no longer served her. Under his guidance, Emily had learned to cultivate a life that was rich in experiences, connections, and joy.

Aaron often reminded her that minimalism was a journey, not a destination. It was a continuous process of evaluation and reflection, of making choices that aligned with her values and brought her closer to her true self. There was no end point, no final achievement—only the ongoing practice of living with intention.

A Global Movement

As Emily delved deeper into the minimalist philosophy, she realized that she was part of a much larger movement. Across the globe, people were awakening to the realization that consumerism was not the path to happiness. They were rejecting the notion that more was better and instead embracing the idea that less could be more—more meaningful, more fulfilling, more aligned with their true desires.

The minimalist movement was gaining momentum, fueled by a growing awareness of the environmental impact of consumer culture and the desire for a more sustainable way of living. People were recognizing that the planet could not sustain the relentless pursuit of more and that a shift towards minimalism could be a powerful force for change.

Emily had become increasingly passionate about the connection between minimalism and sustainability. She saw minimalism as a way to live in harmony with the Earth, to reduce waste and consumption, and to create a more equitable world. It was about recognizing that true wealth was not measured in possessions but in the richness of our experiences and the quality of our relationships.

She had started incorporating these ideas into her workshops, encouraging participants to think about the impact of their choices on the planet and future generations. She spoke about the importance of mindful consumption, of choosing quality over quantity, and of finding joy in the simple pleasures of life.

The Birth of the Minimalist Revolution

One evening, as Emily was preparing for a workshop, she had an idea. What if they could take the minimalist movement to the next level? What if they could create a revolution—a global movement that challenged the status quo and inspired people to rethink their relationship with stuff?

The idea excited her. She imagined a world where people prioritized experiences over possessions, where communities were built on shared values rather than material wealth, and where the planet was treated with respect and care. She saw a world where minimalism was not just a lifestyle choice but a guiding philosophy for a more sustainable and compassionate future.

Emily knew she couldn't do it alone. She reached out to Aaron and a few other key figures in the minimalist community. Together, they began to brainstorm ways to bring the minimalist revolution to life. They decided to launch a campaign that would inspire people to embrace minimalism and challenge the cultural narrative that equated success with material wealth.

They called it The Minimalist Revolution.

The campaign was designed to be inclusive and accessible, inviting people from all walks of life to join the movement. They created a website with resources and tools to help people start their minimalist journey, from decluttering guides to mindfulness exercises and tips for sustainable living. They also launched a social media campaign, sharing stories of people who had transformed their lives through minimalism and encouraging others to do the same.

Emily took on the role of spokesperson for the campaign, using her platform to share her story and inspire others. She spoke at conferences, appeared on podcasts, and wrote articles for major publications, all to spread the message of minimalism far and wide.

A Groundswell of Support

The response was overwhelming. Within weeks, The Minimalist Revolution had gained traction, with thousands of people from around the world joining the movement. Social media was flooded with stories of transformation, with people sharing their experiences of decluttering, simplifying, and living with intention. The hashtag #MinimalistRevolution began trending, and the campaign quickly went viral.

Emily was amazed by the outpouring of support and enthusiasm. She received messages from people who had been inspired to make changes in their own lives, from decluttering their homes to quitting jobs that didn't align with their values. She heard from parents who were teaching their children about the importance of mindful consumption and from young people who were challenging the pressure to conform to consumer culture.

As the movement grew, Emily and her team began to organize events around the world, bringing people together to share their experiences and learn from one another. They held minimalist fairs, where people could swap items they no longer needed, attend workshops on sustainable living, and connect with like-minded individuals. They hosted community clean-ups, promoting the idea that minimalism was not just about personal transformation but also about collective action and responsibility.

The Minimalist Revolution was more than just a campaign—it was a movement that was changing the way people thought about their lives and their impact on the world. It was a call to action, a challenge to rethink the values that had shaped society for so long, and an invitation to create a new way of living that was sustainable, fulfilling, and just.

A Personal Journey

For Emily, the success of The Minimalist Revolution was deeply personal. It was a culmination of her journey, a testament to the power of transformation and the importance of living in alignment with her values. She had started as a young woman overwhelmed by her possessions and dissatisfied with her life, and now she was leading a global movement that was changing the world.

But even as she celebrated the success of the campaign, Emily knew that her journey was far from over. Minimalism was not a destination but a way of being, a continuous practice of living with intention and purpose. She knew that there would always be challenges and temptations, moments of doubt and uncertainty. But she also knew that she had the tools and the community to navigate them.

One evening, as Emily was preparing for another workshop, she received a message from a young woman named Mia. Mia had been following The Minimalist Revolution for several months and had recently started her own minimalist journey. She shared her story of decluttering her apartment, quitting her job to pursue her passion for art, and finding a new sense of purpose and fulfillment.

Mia's message touched Emily deeply. It was a reminder of why she had started this journey in the first place and of the impact that one person could have on the world. She replied to Mia, thanking her for sharing her story and encouraging her to keep going. She knew that Mia was just one of many, that the ripple effect of her transformation was reaching far and wide.

Reflecting on the Journey

As Emily sat down to write her workshop notes, she found herself reflecting on her journey. She thought about the early days of her minimalist experiment, the challenges she had faced, and the lessons she had learned. She remembered the fear and resistance she had felt when she first began letting go and the sense of liberation that had come from embracing a life of simplicity.

She thought about Aaron, who had been her guide and mentor, and all the people she had met along the way who had inspired and supported her. She thought about the countless stories she had heard from people who had transformed their lives through minimalism, each one unique and yet all connected by a common thread of intention and purpose.

Emily realized that The Minimalist Revolution was not just about reducing clutter or living with less. It was about creating a life that was rich in meaning and aligned with one's deepest values. It was about recognizing that happiness and fulfillment came not from what we owned but from who we were and how we lived.

She had learned that minimalism was not a one-size-fits-all solution but a personal journey that looked different for everyone. It was about finding what mattered most to you and making choices that reflected that. It was about letting go of what no longer served you, whether it was physical possessions, toxic relationships, or limiting beliefs, and creating space for what truly mattered.

A Vision for the Future

As The Minimalist Revolution continued to grow, Emily began to think about the future. She dreamed of a world where minimalism was not just a niche lifestyle but a mainstream movement that influenced every aspect of society. She envisioned schools teaching children about the importance of mindful consumption and businesses prioritizing sustainability over profit.

She saw a future where communities were built on shared values and where people came together to support one another in living more intentional, purposeful lives. She imagined a world where the planet was treated with respect and care, where resources were used wisely, and where the well-being of all beings was prioritized over the pursuit of material wealth.

Emily knew that this vision would not be realized overnight. It would take time, effort, and a collective commitment to change. But she also knew that The Minimalist Revolution was just the beginning. It was a spark that had ignited a fire, a catalyst for a new way of thinking and living.

She was filled with a sense of hope and possibility. She believed in the power of individuals to create change, in the strength of community, and in the potential of the human spirit to rise above the challenges of the modern world. She believed that together, they could create a future that was more sustainable, more equitable, and more fulfilling.

A Closing Reflection

As Emily wrapped up her workshop notes, she felt a deep sense of gratitude for the journey she had been on. She was grateful for the challenges and the lessons, for the support and the community, and for the opportunity to make a difference in the world.

She knew that her journey was far from over, that there would always be more to learn and more to explore. But she was excited about the future and the possibilities that lay ahead.

The Minimalist Revolution was just the beginning. It was a call to action, an invitation to live with intention, and a reminder that we all have the power to create change. It was a movement that was transforming lives, communities, and the world.

And Emily was proud to be a part of it.

As she closed her laptop and prepared for the workshop, she took a moment to reflect on how far she had come. She had started with a simple desire to declutter her life, and now she was leading a global movement for change.

She smiled, knowing that this was only the beginning.

The Minimalist Revolution had only just begun.

# Don't miss out!

Visit the website below and you can sign up to receive emails whenever xiaobu publishes a new book. There's no charge and no obligation.

https://books2read.com/r/B-A-FBZIB-XXBAF

BOOKS 2 READ

Connecting independent readers to independent writers.

# About the Author

Archaeologist by day, and a novelist by night, Xiaobu weaves ancient mysteries and forgotten worlds into gripping tales. With a deep passion for history and storytelling, she brings the past to life, blending rich historical detail with compelling narratives that captivate readers and transport them to another time.

Milton Keynes UK
Ingram Content Group UK Ltd.
UKHW030759260924
448894UK00001B/58

9 798227 265845